Exploring Forensics:
Careers for
Curious Minds

- *A Teen's Guide to Forensic Careers*

By,

Shivani Sanger

Exploring Forensics: Careers for Curious Minds: Pathways for Future Careers.

Copyright © Shivani Sanger 2025

DISCLAIMER

As the title suggests, Exploring Forensics: Careers for Curious Minds is a publication designed to enlighten and motivate young adults (aged 13-21) about the career opportunities within forensic science. It is based on thorough research; however, the material (job descriptions, education options, and case studies) is not exhaustive because the field of forensic science continues to change, and the needs in various regions, institutions, and organisations differ.

This book serves as an educational tool, rather than a replacement for professional careers or academic counsel. It encourages readers to seek advice from skilled career counsellors, teachers, or professionals in the field regarding individual guidance on pursuing a career in forensic science. The cases presented are examples.

No liability of the author in connection with the choices taken and the consequences of the use of information presented in this article shall always exist. The responsibility for the use of the material rests squarely on the reader. Any

Exploring Forensics: Careers for Curious Minds: Pathways for Future Careers.

information is provided in its raw format without any guarantees.

No part of this book is to be reproduced or disseminated, and no person can assume the commercial rights of the holders of copyright, and all the material is the sole property of the copyright owner.

Exploring Forensics: Careers for Curious Minds: Pathways for Future Careers.

DEDICATION

I would like to dedicate this book to my loved ones. Without your support, publishing this book would not have been possible.

This book is intended for the next generation of learners and educators who are considering a career in forensic science. May it remind you that breaking new ground is always worth it.

I hope to inspire and empower the next generation of learners and educators, because the future of science belongs to you.

Exploring Forensics: Careers for Curious Minds: Pathways for Future Careers.

ACKNOWLEDGMENTS

I would like to sincerely thank my loved ones for all their support during my academic years.

I would like to extend my particular thanks to a few individuals who have given me guidance, support and encouragement.

Professor. Nikolas Lemos, thank you for the years of endless motivation, support and words of wisdom.

Dr. Laura Fulginiti, thank you for the constant motivation to complete this book and for encouraging me to follow my dreams.

Professor. Fiona Wilcox, thank you for encouraging me to pursue a career in forensic anthropology and for your years of support.

Dr. Matteo Borrini, thank you for motivating me to carry on pursuing my dreams and agreeing to support me through my academic journey.

Exploring Forensics: Careers for Curious Minds: Pathways for Future Careers.

A big thank you to everyone; your belief in me has shaped both my academic journey and this book

Exploring Forensics: Careers for Curious Minds: Pathways for Future Careers.

Table of Contents

PART I: 1

FOUNDATIONS AND HOW TO USE THIS BOOK 1
Welcome and How to Use This Book 1
What exactly is Forensic Science? 2
Where Forensic Evidence Fits in the Justice Process 3
Core Scientific Principles and Chain of Custody 5
Skills and Attributes Across Careers 6
Ethics, Law, Safeguarding and Cultural Sensitivity 8
Study Habits, Wellbeing and Reflective Practice 10
Tools and Technologies You Will Meet 12

PART II 14

THE CAREERS 14

Forensic Anthropology 14
A. Role Overview 14
B. Pathways into the Role 16
C. Case Study 18
D. Word Search 20

Forensic Pathology 22
A. Role Overview 22
B. Pathways into the Role 23
C. Case Study 26
D. Word Search 28

Crime Scene Investigation (CSI/SOCO) 30
A. Role Overview 30
B. Pathways into the Role 32
C. Case Study 34
D. Word Search 37

Exploring Forensics: Careers for Curious Minds: Pathways for Future Careers.

Forensic Biology (DNA and Body Fluids) 39
    A. Role Overview 39
    B. Pathways into the Role 41
    C. Case Study 43
    D. Word Search 46

Forensic Toxicology 48
    A. Role Overview 48
    B. Pathways into the Role 50
    C. Case Study 52
    D. Word Search 55

Forensic Nursing (Sexual Offence and Clinical Roles) 57
    A. Role Overview 57
    B. Pathways into the Role 58
    C. Case Study 60
    D. Word Search 63

Forensic Odontology 65
    A. Role Overview 65
    B. Pathways into the Role 66
    C. Case Study 69
    D. Word Search 70

Forensic Psychology 72
    A. Role Overview 72
    B. Pathways into the Role 74
    C. Case Study 76
    D. Word Search 78

Forensic Accounting 80
    A. Role Overview 80
    B. Pathways into the Role 82
    C. Case Study 84
    D. Word Search 87

Detective Work (Investigative Pathway) 89
    A. Role Overview 89

Exploring Forensics: Careers for Curious Minds: Pathways for Future Careers.

  B. Pathways into the Role 91
  C. Case Study 92

Answers to Word Searches **95**
 Forensic Anthropology 96
 Forensic Pathology 97
 Crime Scene Investigation (CSI/SOCO)Forensic Biology
 Forensic Toxicology 98
 Forensic Nursing 101
 Forensic Odontology 102
 Forensic Psychology 103
 Forensic Accounting 104

PART III: *105*

CAREER LAUNCH AND GROWTH *105*

Building Your Portfolio and Professional Identity **105**
 Finding Roles and Succeeding at Interviews 106
 Continuing Professional Development and Networks 108

PART IV: *109*

CAPSTONE LEARNING TOOLS *109*

Ethical dilemmas for discussion **112**

PART V: *116*

CONCLUSION AND NEXT STEPS *116*

Exploring Forensics: Careers for Curious Minds: Pathways for Future Careers.

PART I:

FOUNDATIONS AND HOW TO USE THIS BOOK

Welcome and How to Use This Book

Curious about the world of forensic science? This book has been designed as a guide for anyone interested in careers in forensic science. Its purpose is to give a clear picture of what each of the professions consists of, how one might go about it, and why it is significant in the broader context of the justice system. By drawing together different specialisms, the book shows the range of opportunities in this field, from laboratory-based jobs to investigative and medical careers.

The structure is very simple. Each career chapter follows the same pattern: a description of the role and what the person does from day to day; how to enter the career, including education, training and qualifications in the UK and the US;

Exploring Forensics: Careers for Curious Minds: Pathways for Future Careers.

and a case study that offers an insight into the role in practice. This consistency provides readers with an easy means of comparison for careers and helps them find information most relevant to their own interests.

The case studies merit special attention. Some are based on true events, whilst others are manufactured examples that reflect common situations. They illustrate the value of forensic expertise and help the reader visualise what professionals really do. Whether you are a student, a parent or just a curious reader, this book is a practical introduction to the world of forensic science.

What exactly is Forensic Science?

Forensic science is the application of scientific knowledge to the affairs of the law. The term "forensic" itself dates from the Latin forensic, meaning "of the forum" which was, in the past, the space for public debate and judgement. In the modern era, it denotes the use of science in supporting legal processes, in ensuring that decisions are made on verifiable facts, rather than assumptions or speculation.

The discipline extensively utilises the scientific method. This consists of the meticulous observation of evidence, the

Exploring Forensics: Careers for Curious Minds: Pathways for Future Careers.

construction of hypotheses, and the testing of hypotheses through repeatable procedures. Whether the subject is a blood sample, a financial record or a psychological assessment, the goal is to apply rigorous analysis that yields reliable findings. In this way, forensic science develops results that can withstand a cross-examination test in a court.

Central to the field is reliability. Courts require objective, consistent, and independent evidence. Forensic science addresses this demand by providing results which can be validated by peers and reproduced under the same conditions. This is why forensic scientists not only need to be proficient in their technical skills, but they must also maintain stringent ethical standards. Their work is the basis on which just outcomes can be achieved.

Where Forensic Evidence Fits in the Justice Process

Forensic evidence passes through a number of stages before it reaches a courtroom. The process begins at the crime scene or the scene of such an incident, with investigators carefully picking up and recording items that may have significance. These may be biological traces, physical impressions, digital

Exploring Forensics: Careers for Curious Minds: Pathways for Future Careers.

traces, or chemical substances. The state of the evidence recovered is of paramount importance as errors at this stage can make it less valuable in later proceedings.

Once collected, evidences are transferred to forensic labs or specialised examiners. Here, scientists analyse the materials through established techniques. DNA samples may be profiled, fingerprints compared, or toxic substances identified. Each test is conducted under strict protocols in order to ensure integrity and prevent contamination. At times, coroners and pathologists are also involved, especially when a death is to be investigated to ascertain the cause of death.

The findings are then compiled in the form of formal reports. These reports are conveyed to police, prosecutors and defence teams as part of the legal disclosure process. They are the factual basis on which decisions about charges and trial strategy are made. At trial, forensic experts may be called to give evidence of their findings and to explain their methods. Their testimony helps to educate the judges and juries about the importance of scientific evidence in the larger context of the case.

Forensic science, therefore, does not work independently, but works in conjunction with the police officers, lawyers and courts. Its value lies in making the situation clear and certain, and in creating evidence from scattered information for the pursuit of justice.

Core Scientific Principles and Chain of Custody

At the core of forensic science is the preservation of the evidence in the state it was found in. This all begins with showing awareness of contamination risk. A deviation from protocol, even in the most minor way, such as handling the samples without wearing gloves or exposure to environmental conditions, may affect the quality of the experimental results. For this reason, scientists and investigators adhere to strict procedures that ensure the evidence remains free from cross-contamination and also that the validity of the evidence is never lost as it progresses.

Everything must be properly recorded. A record must be kept of what, where, who and in what conditions it was found. Photographs and notes are used for additional evidence, forming an open trail which can be examined at any time. Packaging is equally important. Biological samples can be stored in sterile containers; firearms sealed in tamper-proof bags, and documents preserved in conditions that do not allow them to deteriorate.

This process creates what's called the chain of custody. It assures continuity by demonstrating that evidence has been in safekeeping since it was collected until it is produced in court. Each transfer is recorded, thus providing accountability and trust in the integrity of the material.

Quality assurance is the basis for all of this. Laboratories are working under standards such as ISO 17025, which require tight controls over testing procedures and calibration of equipment. Apart from providing assurance that results are produced in internationally recognised conditions, these frameworks also provide courts with confidence that they are based on scientifically sound methodology without such strong standards, evidence may be easily challenged and dismissed.

Skills and Attributes Across Careers

Think you have what it takes to be in this field? Let's find out.

While each forensic career requires its own specialist knowledge, there are some core skills and attributes that are

Exploring Forensics: Careers for Curious Minds: Pathways for Future Careers.

common throughout the field. Observation is a major requirement. The skill to observe small details such as slight marks on a surface or inconsistencies in an account often can make a difference between success and failure.

Critical thinking is just as necessary. Forensic professionals have to consider evidence objectively and consider a variety of possibilities before reaching conclusions. This requires a disciplined approach that is resistant to personal bias and that relies solely on tested methods. Written reporting is another global skill. Courts depend on understandable, well-written documentation that summarises findings simply and without sacrificing accuracy. Poorly expressed reports may undermine even the best evidence.

Courtroom communication is an extension of this requirement. Forensic experts have to be ready to convey complex science to judges and juries clearly and confidently. They have to keep their head under cross-examination and maintain their professional integrity while making sure that their evidence is understood.

Ethics are the foundation for all forensic work. Scientists and investigators must be impartial and serve truth, not interest or external pressure. Paralleled with ethics is resilience. Many roles involve encountering distressing material,

Exploring Forensics: Careers for Curious Minds: Pathways for Future Careers.

whether through the examination of human remains, the examination of the evidence for an incident of violence, or the tracing of financial crimes with devastating human consequences. Professionals are required to handle these pressures but still maintain objectivity.

Together, these skills and attributes characterised the forensic community. They ensure that in spite of the variety of roles, practitioners have a common foundation to fulfil their role in serving the justice system effectively.

Ethics, Law, Safeguarding and Cultural Sensitivity

Forensic science does not exist in isolation from other areas of practice, and at its heart is a responsibility to act in accordance with ethical principles, legal frameworks and respect for the rights and dignity of human beings. These responsibilities permeate all professional roles and are an integral part of the handling of evidence and the care of all involved parties.

The care of victims constitutes a field of special importance. Forensic nurses, psychologists, and investigators often have direct interaction with people who have been harmed.

Exploring Forensics: Careers for Curious Minds: Pathways for Future Careers.

Consent must be given in all cases before either examinations or interviews. The procedures should be carried out in such an empathic way as to acknowledge the vulnerability of the affected parties. Safeguarding measures are put in place to protect the victims from further harm in order to ensure that the welfare of the victim is put above the insistence of justice.

Data protection is another basic principle of ethical practice. The information that is processed in forensic activities is often very sensitive information, for example medical records, financial accounts, or genetic information. Confidentiality must therefore be maintained at all times. Breaches of confidentiality undermine trust and can lead to legal penalties; therefore, robust information security systems and stringent access controls are necessary.

Cultural sensitivity is also an important consideration. Forensic anthropologists may be expected to work with human remains that come from various communities, where cultural or religious customs determine how these remains are treated. Similarly, forensic nurses may encounter victims from different backgrounds, in which different perceptions of healthcare, gender roles or authority prevail. Sensitivity in such contexts is indispensable if respect and cooperation are to be preserved and encouraged.

Impartiality is central to all the aforementioned concerns. Forensic professionals are bound by the ethics not to be prejudiced in their work, to refrain from making assumptions on the basis of race, gender, religion or social status. No longer is the prosecutor or the judge accountable to personal belief or external compulsion, but only to the evidence and the striving for justice.

By promoting a balance of ethical behaviour, legal practices, protocols for safeguards and cultural sensitivity, forensic science helps to cement its credibility. This holistic approach ensures that the discipline is not only relevant to the courts but also to the wider society, fostering fairness and respect.

Study Habits, Wellbeing and Reflective Practice

Success in forensic science is not only a result of technical skill, but also result of disciplined study habits and personal wellbeing. Time management is a valuable tool for balancing the needs of lectures, casework, and independent study for students and professionals. It helps to avoid the stress of last minute, as planning tasks in advance and breaking down

Exploring Forensics: Careers for Curious Minds: Pathways for Future Careers.

projects into smaller stages ensures the project gets moved along at a steady pace.

Note-keeping is also another important habit. Accurate and organised notes provide reference at the time of assessments and professional practice. Many forensic scientists keep reflective logs in which they record what they have learnt, challenges faced, and how they overcame them. These reflections provide evidence of deeper critical thinking and evidence of professional growth.

Supervision is a key aspect of learning. Regular meetings with tutors, mentors or senior colleagues are a source of guidance, feedback and reassurance. In professional practise, supervision also ensures that the complex or sensitive cases are approached with proper supervision.

Exposure to disturbing content is an integral part of forensic work. Crime scene, abuse scene, or violence scenes can be very hard to digest. Forensic scholars and professionals need to establish coping strategies, seek support as necessary, and identify professional and personal boundaries. Attentive self- care is the key to having a long and effective career.

Exploring Forensics: Careers for Curious Minds: Pathways for Future Careers.

Tools and Technologies You Will Meet

Forensic science is based on a vast array of equipment and technologies developed to collect, store, and analyse evidence. Personal protective equipment (PPE) is one of the most fundamental but indispensable tools. Gloves, masks and protective suits are needed to prevent evidence contamination and to protect the health of investigators working in dangerous conditions.

Scene kits are transported to a location where incidents have occurred. These generally include fingerprint powders, swabs, evidence bags, scales for photography and markers for labelling. Their purpose is to make sure that evidence is properly recovered and kept for later analysis.

DNA platforms are becoming an integral part of modern forensic biology within analysis laboratories. These instruments allow scientists to extract, amplify and profile genetic material with precision. In toxicology, special devices such as gas chromatographs and mass spectrometers are used for the detection and measurement of drugs, poisons and other substances in biological matrices.

Imaging technologies are also important. X-rays, CT scans and digital photography help forensic anthropologists,

Exploring Forensics: Careers for Curious Minds: Pathways for Future Careers.

pathologists and odontologists investigate remains and injuries without invasive procedures. In the digital age, forensic experts also use computer-based tools to address casework. Software is used for data analysis, evidence tracking and event reconstruction.

These technologies are constantly evolving as science and industry make advances. Forensic professionals need to be adaptable, and also learn to use new instruments as they emerge. Mastery of these tools means that evidence is handled accurately, securely, and in an appropriate manner to ensure reliable conclusions in court.

Exploring Forensics: Careers for Curious Minds: Pathways for Future Careers.

PART II

THE CAREERS

Forensic Anthropology

A. Role Overview

Forensic anthropology is the application of human skeletal remains to the field of law. Its primary use is for identifying the deceased and reconstructing events at the time of death in cases where only bones or bone fragments have been preserved. By examining the skeleton, forensic anthropologists make estimates of age, sex, ancestry, stature, and other unique features that can aid in identification. This process is known as creating a biological profile.

Osteological science is the basis for the discipline. Injuries or pathological changes of interest in the development of aetiology or manner of death can be recognised by the anthropologist who has a well-developed understanding of skeletal morphology. Criminal autopsies are an important task, and they include determining whether the death was caused by an injury that occurred before the body cooled, at

Exploring Forensics: Careers for Curious Minds: Pathways for Future Careers.

the moment of death, or after the body cooled. Such analyses may provide information on violence, accidents, or post-mortem injury.

Taphonomy, the scientific study of post-mortem processes that act on fossilised remains, is also a main theme. Forensic anthropologists determine the impact of the decomposition process, as well as factors such as burial, the activity of fauna, and environmental exposure, on bones. The analysis of the internal anatomy of the human remains is valuable as a tool for estimating the time of death and reconstructing the circumstances in which the remains were found.

In cases of mass mortality caused by natural disasters or war, forensic anthropologists play an important role in identifying the deceased. Doing regular work with archaeologists during controlled recovery operations to ensure contextual integrity is maintained. While their field is bounded by ignorance, for example, bones may be fragmented, poorly preserved or contaminated, and some conclusions are inevitably equivocal. Nevertheless, forensic anthropology is a strong source of evidence based upon scientific observation for the purpose of judicial proceedings.

Exploring Forensics: Careers for Curious Minds: Pathways for Future Careers.

B. Pathways into the Role

In the United Kingdom, the forensic anthropological vocational path is generally initiated at secondary school through higher-level study of biology, chemistry or other related science subjects. Students then go on to study for a Bachelor of Science degree in anthropology, archaeology or a similar discipline. Particularly beneficial is when the program is accredited by the Chartered Society of Forensic Sciences (CSFS). A postgraduate level is usually required, and a Master's degree in forensic anthropology or osteoarchaeology enables higher-level training in skeletal analysis, trauma, and recovery methodologies. Some scholars go on to doctoral-level research where they specialise in a niche, for example, paleopathology or taphonomical investigations. Certification routes, such as those offered by the Royal Anthropological Institute (RAI) or the Forensic Anthropological Society of Europe (FASE), provide recognition of competence and are highly valued in practice.

Professional bodies give structure and credence. Membership in organisations such as the British Association for Forensic Anthropology (BAFA) provides networking, mentoring, and access to best practices. Practical training is

Exploring Forensics: Careers for Curious Minds: Pathways for Future Careers.

often acquired by excavation projects, recovery exercises and placements with museum or archaeological units. Developing research skills is also necessary, as forensic anthropology is a discipline that is continually evolving with new studies in the sciences. With experience, practitioners may be called as expert witnesses in court, presenting findings on identity or trauma.

In the United States, students usually start with a Bachelor's degree in Anthropology or Biology. Many then undertake Master's or doctoral programmes in Forensic Anthropology, where advanced laboratory and field training is emphasised. Field schools are a large component, with hands-on opportunities for excavation and recovery. Certification routes, including those offered by the American Board of Forensic Anthropology (ABFA), are recognised for their validation of competence and are highly valued in practice.

Progression in both countries often involves a mix of teaching, research and casework. Other forensic anthropologists divide their time between teaching and working as consultants at law enforcement agencies. Good practices and commitment are fostered through volunteering in museums or recovery teams. Finally, the job demands continuous professional growth, not necessarily to remain technically current, but also to achieve the standard of credibility necessary in a legal environment.

C. Case Study

During the construction of a new housing development, an employee discovered a mass of bones. The area was cordoned off by local police, and a forensic anthropologist was called on to oversee the recovery. In collaboration with archaeologists, the team thoroughly recorded the surroundings, stratification of the soil, artefacts, and the location of each bone. To reduce contamination, standard procedures were used, and to preserve associations of remains with the environment.

In the laboratory, the anthropologist carefully reconstructed the skeleton, a standard step in forensic anthropology called *reassociation*. Analysis showed the remains were of a middle-aged man, estimated at about 40–50 years old based on dental wear and changes in the pubic symphysis. The biological profile suggested European ancestry, with an estimated stature of approximately 6 feet (183 cm), calculated from long bone measurements using statistical methods. Several healed rib fractures showed signs of *callus*

Exploring Forensics: Careers for Curious Minds: Pathways for Future Careers.

formation, evidence of injuries that had mended years before death. Closer examination of the skull revealed sharp-force trauma, likely caused by a bladed weapon such as a sword or axe, leaving V-shaped cut marks characteristic of such injuries. Radiocarbon dating of the bone collagen suggested death had occurred several centuries earlier, long before modern records were kept.

Although there was no direct match that could be made with the missing persons, the case served as a good demonstration of the role that forensic anthropology plays in both historical and legal enquiries. The recovery protocols emphasised the importance of context, whereas the trauma assessment provided insight into the manner of death.

Exploring Forensics: Careers for Curious Minds: Pathways for Future Careers.

D. Word Search

Each puzzle contains important words from this chapter. They might be hidden forwards, backwards, up, down, or diagonally. Just like real investigations, you'll need to look carefully!

See if you can find all the words and challenge a friend to beat your time.

Exploring Forensics: Careers for Curious Minds: Pathways for Future Careers.

Forensic Anthropology Word Search

```
J  I  D  E  N  T  I  F  I  C  A  T  I  O  N  U  B  S  Q  S
D  E  Y  Z  N  B  B  K  S  D  X  H  F  U  H  I  L  A  T  G
R  O  P  A  T  H  O  L  O  G  Y  A  E  C  D  W  F  B  N  M
N  E  E  S  W  O  S  L  L  A  B  O  R  A  T  O  R  Y  K  M
Q  L  R  R  F  O  H  P  C  R  G  S  A  J  N  K  X  X  E  V
R  I  M  E  X  U  O  X  T  G  E  T  J  C  B  N  E  Q  E  N
J  F  F  T  M  S  K  E  L  E  T  O  N  D  N  B  Y  U  G  C
J  O  R  S  D  E  C  O  M  P  O  S  I  T  I  O  N  N  P  F
U  R  K  A  I  J  T  H  Z  B  S  V  P  K  Y  D  D  C  O  S
I  P  S  S  W  L  Y  Q  J  D  Y  T  B  M  R  I  B  I  T  W
O  L  U  I  U  U  G  Y  L  O  Z  L  O  R  R  M  I  K  D  A
U  A  C  D  Y  N  S  P  I  R  T  N  F  D  M  N  J  D  T  E
C  C  X  S  J  I  C  G  I  E  O  Q  E  Z  H  T  B  G  X  L
K  I  P  S  K  M  V  J  T  H  H  H  M  A  X  P  I  E  H  X
V  G  I  A  O  H  A  E  P  O  D  B  X  G  K  N  Q  J  I  K
H  O  M  M  V  I  W  A  Y  E  A  O  K  Z  T  F  D  B  I  F
N  L  M  R  B  U  T  Q  A  D  U  I  V  G  D  Q  T  W  Q  N
P  O  H  A  T  K  B  T  R  A  U  M  A  Z  C  Y  J  S  V  Q
H  I  G  A  R  C  H  A  E  O  L  O  G  I  S  T  S  I  E  L
C  B  V  B  M  I  P  W  B  M  A  D  X  M  M  H  Z  Y  G  X
```

- o Mass Disasters
- o Skeleton
- o Identification
- o Biological Profile
- o Taphonomy
- o Decomposition
- o Archaeologists
- o Pathology
- o Laboratory
- o Trauma

Exploring Forensics: Careers for Curious Minds: Pathways for Future Careers.

Forensic Pathology

A. Role Overview

Forensic pathology is the branch of medicine that examines death in circumstances that are sudden, unexpected or suspicious. The central practice is the autopsy, a methodical examination of the body with the intent of establishing the cause and manner of death. The cause of death is the particular injury, disease, or substance which brought about a death, whereas the manner of death is the classification of the death as natural, accidental, suicidal, homicide, or undetermined.

A forensic pathologist is trained to deduce precise interpretations of injuries. Patterns of trauma are reviewed in relation to their probable aetiology. Blunt-force injuries can indicate assault, road traffic collision or accidental fall. Sharp-force wounds may be indicative of stabbing or cutting instruments. Gunshot wounds are evaluated with respect to range, trajectory and sequence. In addition, natural disease processes such as cardiac failure or stroke are assessed to rule out non-violent causes.

Sample selection is a vital responsibility. Tissues and fluids are sampled for histological and toxicological examination.

Exploring Forensics: Careers for Curious Minds: Pathways for Future Careers.

Histology (the study of tissue under the microscope) can uncover hidden disease or subtle injuries. Toxicology identifies drugs, poisons, or chemicals that may have contributed to death. The forensic pathologist guarantees that proper samples are collected and safeguarded for proper laboratory evaluation.

Liaison is a daily aspect of the role. Pathologists liaise with police investigators, coroners or procurators fiscal to match the medical findings with evidence from the scene. They also meet with the families of the deceased, providing explanations with sensitivity and objectivity. Courtroom testimony is another extension of this responsibility, requiring clear communication of complex medical facts.

B. Pathways into the Role

In the United Kingdom, the route to becoming a forensic pathologist typically begins with a medical degree, which usually lasts five years. Upon completing the degree, doctors undergo two years of Foundation training (F1 and F2), during which they are exposed to various medical specialities. Aspiring pathologists then go on to train in histopathology, a process that typically takes five years. This

Exploring Forensics: Careers for Curious Minds: Pathways for Future Careers.

includes the study of disease in tissues, the interpretation of biopsies, and post-mortem examination.

Within this training, some doctors decide to specialise in forensic histopathology, a recognised subspecialty that deals with deaths that require investigation by the law. This includes specialist placements, advanced autopsy training and exposure to court processes. Membership in the Royal College of Pathologists is the next step in professional development and is achieved through examinations that assess both scientific knowledge and practical ability. In the UK, forensic pathologists belong to the coronial system and are trained to investigate an unexplained or violent death at the request of the coroner.

In the United States, the process tends to be more similar across different organisations. Once medical school and the MD or DO degree have been completed, physicians enter a pathology residency. This training typically spans four years, encompassing both anatomical and clinical pathology. Following the residency, candidates are required to undergo a one-year fellowship in forensic pathology, during which they receive comprehensive training in the medicolegal aspects of death investigation. The standard of certification is board certification through the American Board of

Exploring Forensics: Careers for Curious Minds: Pathways for Future Careers.

Pathology, which is a certification of professional competence. In the US, forensic pathologists often serve within county or state medical examiner systems, and are also major participants in the investigation of sudden deaths.

In both nations, experience in court exposure and report writing is required in the position. Reports should be well summarised, precise, and presented in clear and understandable language. Cooperation with other fields is frequent, e.g., with anthropology when dealing with skeletal cases, with odontology when dealing with dental identifications, and with toxicology when dealing with chemical analysis. Working in multiple disciplines ensures that the findings are thorough and pass the legal test.

Medicine, science, and law are closely related and make the career challenging. Its appeal to those who are drawn to it lies in its service to society: it represents the dead, safeguards the health of citizens, and furnishes evidence in support of justice.

The career is challenging yet offers a unique blend of medicine, science, and law. Those attracted to it often appreciate its contributions to society: speaking for the dead, protecting public health, and providing evidence that supports justice.

C. Case Study

An 89-year-old man was found dead in his house. There were no witnesses to his final hours, and the scene presented mixed findings. The furniture was disturbed, suggesting a likelihood of a fall or struggle. The body had bruises on the torso and a laceration to the scalp. The first thing that was recorded was whether the death was the result of natural disease, accident, or foul play.

At autopsy, both external and internal features were examined by the forensic pathologist. The scalp laceration was determined to be the result of a fall against furniture and not a weapon. Small red pinpoint spots, known as *petechiae*, were also noted on the eyelids. Petechiae occur when tiny blood vessels break, and they can appear in cases of suffocation, strangulation, or heart failure. Internal examination found major narrowing of the coronary arteries, consistent with advanced heart disease. Microscopic histology revealed an acute myocardial infarction, showing that the deceased had suffered a heart attack.

Exploring Forensics: Careers for Curious Minds: Pathways for Future Careers.

Toxicological analysis was also performed. Blood and urine specimens provided evidence of therapeutic levels of prescribed medication, excluding overdose or poisoning. The bruising on the torso was considered consistent with collapsing during the heart attack rather than assault. Correlation with the scene supported this interpretation, since there were no signs of forced entry or theft.

In court, the pathologist presented these findings. Using plain language, they explained that the cause of death was a natural heart attack, with injuries sustained as a consequence of collapse. The death was therefore classified as *natural*. The explanation brought closure to the family and clarity to investigators, demonstrating how forensic pathology separates suspicion from certainty.

Exploring Forensics: Careers for Curious Minds: Pathways for Future Careers.

D. Word Search

Each puzzle contains important words from this chapter. They might be hidden forwards, backwards, up, down, or diagonally. Just like real investigations, you'll need to look carefully!

See if you can find all the words and challenge a friend to beat your time.

Exploring Forensics: Careers for Curious Minds: Pathways for Future Careers.

Forensic Pathology Word Search

```
J R S Q L O F L O O Y P S U N B A K V D
Z B D F E G N R N Q H F C S U Q M I D L
B V Y L M X E F D V A O S I D R U N K L
I A J B B N P G A K G Q L U I M N G I P
A S S V O U A U I K D W O K T Y B Q A T
R H W R T O X I C O L O G Y Z B K Y K J
T Z O Y H P R H P P B S R M H F Q Y E B
S C Y V T F D Q F G C B R W U L F M X I
I A U C A M I C R O S C O P E K U W Q O
G F O R E N S I C P A T H O L O G Y R P
O I D W D W H O P H I S T O L O G Y R B
L N J D F S G G B Z M S L N K I U S P A
O F M L O E X I H J O Y J T Q U S K M C
H R L S R S A W B V O S L W Q P U U P S
T K P W E O J U L F R P W M E Y A Q J Y
A Z F C N H Y G P X T O U P A R H L O B
P P L P N H M B G D R T J Q T A Y D F A
H L T C A O I V C H U U P K A R J L R Z
P X U N M V L B H P O A X Q J M T M Y V
H N D O L O B S E J C B K E Y N C P O G
```

- o Forensic Pathology
- o Autopsy
- o Manner Of Death
- o Pathologist
- o Trauma
- o Histology
- o Toxicology
- o Coroner
- o Courtroom
- o Microscope

Exploring Forensics: Careers for Curious Minds: Pathways for Future Careers.

Crime Scene Investigation (CSI/SOCO)

A. Role Overview

The forensic process usually begins with Crime Scene Investigation. Crime Scene Investigators (CSIs) or, in the United Kingdom, Scenes of Crime Officers (SOCOs) have the responsibility of securing, documenting, and collecting evidence at the scene of the occurrence. Their job is to ensure that all relevant material is preserved, recorded, and presented so that it is reliable and admissible in court.

The first obligation of a CSI is to secure the scene. This includes setting up boundaries, limiting access and avoiding contamination. Once secured, the scene is systematically recorded. Photography, sketches, and detailed notes capture the environment as it is found. These records offer an enduring account of the conditions, enabling investigators, lawyers and juries to visualise the setting long after it has been cleared.

The work focuses on recognising evidence. CSIs also receive training to identify those things that would not have been noticeable to the untrained eye but are essential in the procedure of linking the suspects to the crime. These may

Exploring Forensics: Careers for Curious Minds: Pathways for Future Careers.

include fingerprints, biological prints (such as blood, saliva, and footwear prints). Latent prints or trace materials that are invisible to the naked eye can be brought to light by special methods, such as chemical enhancement or other sources of alternate light.

Once they have been identified, the evidence must be carefully gathered. Each item is carefully packaged to maintain its integrity, and strict attention is given to continuity and documentation. Tamper-proof bags, sterile swabs and labelled containers all play a role in this process. The packaging not only serves as a protective measure for the evidence itself, but it can also ensure that the evidence can be traced back to every stage of handling.

A CSI's work doesn't end at the scene. They may be called to court to explain their methods and results. Their testimony is useful to juries in understanding how evidence was discovered, preserved, and connected to the larger investigation. The role is thus both pragmatic and communicative, requiring both scientific ability, attention to detail and confidence under pressure.

Exploring Forensics: Careers for Curious Minds: Pathways for Future Careers.

B. Pathways into the Role

In the United Kingdom, most CSIs work as members of the police force (but not as sworn police officers). Entry requirements vary between forces, but typically a combination of qualifications and practical aptitude is required by candidates. While a degree isn't compulsory, many applicants study forensic investigation, biology or criminology at undergraduate or diploma level to enhance their profile. Most CSI jobs in the United Kingdom require you to complete a CSI course from a United Kingdom-based provider. Once recruited, training is imparted through the College of Policing or internal force programmes. This training includes evidence recovery, photography, health and safety and legal procedures.

Competency frameworks help to guide professional development. CSIs often start out in junior positions and learn to manage routine cases before moving up to senior positions where they manage complex or serious cases such as homicides. Specialisation may also be a part of career progression, e.g. footwear marks, blood pattern analysis or recording digital scenes. Continuous training helps keep staff familiar with new methods and legislative changes.

Exploring Forensics: Careers for Curious Minds: Pathways for Future Careers.

In the United States, there are different pathways into CSI roles, depending on whether the position is an embedded role in the police force or a civilian post. Some agencies employ sworn police officers as CSIs, while others hire civilian staff with specialised scientific training. A Bachelor's degree in forensic science, criminal justice, or a related field is common, and many states operate training academies for evidence technicians and CSIs.

Certification can help to build credibility. The International Association for Identification (IAI) offers certification in the areas of crime scene analysis and fingerprint examination. While these are not always mandatory, such credentials serve as a testament to a commitment to standards and professional excellence. Entry-level positions, such as evidence technician or assistant CSI, offer a foundation that can progress to lead investigator positions with additional experience.

Across both the UK and the US, the role requires flexibility. CSIs work shifts, including nights and weekends and are sometimes called out at short notice to attend to major incidents. Health and safety considerations pervade, as investigators may be confronted with hazardous environments, biohazards or dangerous substances. Precise record-keeping and report writing are also essential, as all that will be undertaken at the scene must be explained in written statements.

The career suits those who demonstrate a complex scientific interest, a detail-oriented approach, and the ability to remain stable in stressful situations. It provides a unique opportunity to make a direct contribution to justice by piecing together seemingly small fragments of evidence that may alter the direction of investigations.

C. Case Study

A suburban neighbourhood had been hit by a series of burglaries. At one house, a CSI carried out a detailed examination to look for traces the offender had left behind.

The first step was to secure and photograph the scene before touching anything. Careful documentation helps show the court exactly how the scene looked.

On a windowsill, the CSI developed *latent fingerprints*. Since the surface was smooth glass, they used fingerprint powder and a brush to make the ridges visible. (Powder

Exploring Forensics: Careers for Curious Minds: Pathways for Future Careers.

clings to natural oils and sweat in fingerprints.) The best prints were photographed and then lifted using adhesive tape before being sealed in evidence bags. In some cases, CSIs may also use *superglue fuming (cyanoacrylate)* in a controlled chamber to make prints appear on glass or plastic.

Near the point of entry, a small *blood smear* was visible on broken glass. The CSI collected the stain using a sterile swab, which was packaged in a tamper-proof evidence container. This type of sample would later be sent for *DNA profiling*, a process in which short sections of genetic code (*STR*s, or short tandem repeats) are compared to those of known individuals in police databases.

On the carpet, the CSI also noticed *footwear impressions*. Using *gel lifters* (sticky sheets designed to capture delicate marks), the impressions were preserved. Back at the lab, the patterns could be compared to known databases of shoe soles. If needed, casts can also be made for 3D printing from objects found outdoors in soil.

Every step was logged in detail to maintain the *chain of custody*. This ensures evidence is admissible in court and cannot be challenged as mishandled.

Exploring Forensics: Careers for Curious Minds: Pathways for Future Careers.

The lab results confirmed that the DNA matched an offender already in the national database for burglary. The fingerprints were also linked to the same person, and the footwear impressions provided further supporting evidence.

Within days, the police made an arrest. In court, the CSI described how the fingerprints, DNA, and footwear impressions had been carefully collected and explained how these independent lines of evidence all pointed to the same suspect.

Exploring Forensics: Careers for Curious Minds: Pathways for Future Careers.

D. Word Search

Each puzzle contains important words from this chapter. They might be hidden forwards, backwards, up, down, or diagonally. Just like real investigations, you'll need to look carefully!

See if you can find all the words and challenge a friend to beat your time.

Exploring Forensics: Careers for Curious Minds: Pathways for Future Careers.

Crime Scene Investigation Word Search

```
K R T E S T I M O N Y L G O N J O T G H
B L O O D S P L A T T E R O U C Q Q Y K
A P K H R R Z W G X I E I I X N S Y V P
O W X D J S V W L E V T I Y S A J A X G
I F H T W L M V T X A C B R D X Z W Z E
L U Z J N V I H S T V D O E G X B S K X
M Q U Z X F C K N B E T M D V O M S Y Y
S E L K W U R E N T A Y E V O O S U J U
W C U N F H M Y V G H I F K M R O T R N
E N G A T U Q U I P R Q E O Y Z M E J W
Y E Q M C K L T A Q T H G G X X Z V G P
M D B O E R S R G V Z J B A R H V M U F
B I D G J E G C V A W G B W D S G P H A
F V F X V O B F I N G E R P R I N T S I
N E J N T O F M M C C R I M E S C E N E
S L I O P J E O E G Z E N Y V U R A W W
M N H S E Z J Z P Z M Q L V P G V D S Q
M P M X C O N T A M I N A T I O N N D N
K E G R Z A G R N T G K K B L D D D T S
D U P G L W I Y P A C K A G I N G A N N
```

- Crime Scene Investigators
- Evidence
- Contamination
- Fingerprints
- Blood Splatter
- Documentation
- Packaging
- Testimony
- Photography

Exploring Forensics: Careers for Curious Minds: Pathways for Future Careers.

Forensic Biology (DNA and Body Fluids)

A. Role Overview

Forensic biology focuses on the analysis of DNA and body fluids to present as evidence in criminal and civil cases. Its most recognised tool is DNA profiling, the comparison of genetic material from crime scenes to reference samples. A profile may place a suspect at a crime scene, link cases together, or exonerate an innocent person. Unlike fingerprints, DNA analysis can be conducted on very small or degraded samples, making it invaluable in modern investigations.

Interpreting mixtures is one of the most complicated problems in the field. Many times, there is DNA from more than one person in a sample, such as in cases of assault. Forensic biologists must separate these profiles, assigning probabilities to the various contributors. This requires sophisticated statistical modelling and a bit of judgment, especially if the data is partial or unclear.

Identifying body fluids is another important duty. Scientists may have to verify if a stain is blood, semen, saliva, or something else. Such identifications can provide support for

Exploring Forensics: Careers for Curious Minds: Pathways for Future Careers.

the reconstruction of events and point to further testing. Presumptive and confirmatory tests are employed, each with its own reliability and limitations.

Reporting is key to the role. Forensic biologists not only present results but also explain their meaning. They frequently report results in terms of probabilities: for example, stating that a DNA profile is a billion times more likely to have come from a suspect than from an unknown individual. This helps courts to be aware of the strength of the evidence without overstating certainty.

Contamination control is extremely important throughout. Laboratories have very exacting protocols to avoid cross-contamination from one sample to another. Staff use protective clothing, work in controlled environments and monitor background DNA levels. Even so, limitations exist. Profiles can be incomplete, statistics can be misinterpreted, and the transfer of DNA does not necessarily demonstrate contact at the time of a crime. Forensic biologists must therefore combine a technical skill with honesty about uncertainty.

Exploring Forensics: Careers for Curious Minds: Pathways for Future Careers.

B. Pathways into the Role

In the United Kingdom, forensic biology is typically studied as part of a degree in Biology or Forensic Science. Accredited degrees in the Chartered Society of Forensic Sciences (CSFS) are particularly desirable because they address the critical competencies. Practical experience in NHS or non-NHS laboratory placements within the study introduces the students to evidence manipulation and its prevention, as well as the analytical methods

After graduation, new graduates can begin their careers in technical positions within forensic laboratories. These positions involve preparing samples and conducting routine tests, and assisting senior staff. Competence is obtained under the rigorous frameworks of ISO-accredited laboratories, where the validation of every method and process must be thoroughly documented. As experience accumulates, practitioners may advance to a status of reporting scientist. At this level, they interpret results, draft statements for the court and testify as expert witnesses.

Training is continuous. Reporting scientists must not only learn technical skills, but also how to communicate in a courtroom, write reports in a way that presents statistics in a way that can be easily understood, and testify in a manner

Exploring Forensics: Careers for Curious Minds: Pathways for Future Careers.

that can be received by judges and juries. This is significantly facilitated through mentoring by seniors. Professional organisations, such as the CSFS, are also beneficial in terms of membership, which provides networking and additional professional development opportunities.

In the United States, the route runs along a similar path but with its own structure. A Bachelor's degree in Biology, Chemistry, or Forensic Science gives the foundation. Many laboratories favour applicants who have coursework in genetics, molecular biology, and biochemistry. Once recruited, training is conducted under proven training methods with quality systems often unique to state or federal laboratories. Competence is evaluated by periodic auditing and proficiency testing.

Progression usually goes from analysis at the bench level to interpretation and reporting. Some types of biologists specialise in specific types of evidence, such as sexual assault kits or complex mixtures. As they advance, they may be qualified to present the results of their findings in court as expert witnesses. There are certification options, such as the American Board of Criminalistics, that help to enhance credibility.

Exploring Forensics: Careers for Curious Minds: Pathways for Future Careers.

Across the UK and the US, the career requires tenacity and accuracy. The workload is often sensitive cases, such as sexual assaults, homicides or child abuse. Exposure to such material not only requires emotional strength but also technical expertise. The payoff is the contribution to justice that results from providing evidence of sufficient scientific rigour and legal significance.

C. Case Study

A sexual assault kit was turned in to the forensic laboratory after an attack was reported. The forensic biologist first checked the *chain of custody*, confirming that the seals on the evidence were intact and the documentation was complete. This process ensures the samples have been securely handled from the point of collection all the way to analysis.

The first step in the laboratory was *screening for body fluids*. Swabs and clothing were tested using *presumptive tests* that can indicate the possible presence of semen. For example, the *acid phosphatase test* reacts quickly with enzymes found in seminal fluid, producing a colour change. A positive result

Exploring Forensics: Careers for Curious Minds: Pathways for Future Careers.

was then confirmed using a *microscopic examination for sperm cells* and a *prostate-specific antigen (p30/PSA) test*.

With the presence of semen confirmed, the biologist selected the best sample for *DNA profiling*. Standard laboratory methods were used:

- **DNA extraction** (removing DNA from cells in the stain),
- **Quantification** (measuring how much DNA is present),
- **Amplification** (using *PCR*, polymerase chain reaction, to make many copies of target DNA regions)
- **STR profiling** (analysing short tandem repeats, the markers used in forensic DNA typing).

A complete DNA profile was generated and compared with the national offender database. It matched an individual with past convictions. The *random match probability* (the chance of another unrelated person having the same profile) was calculated as less than one in a billion.

The forensic biologist carefully explained their findings in the report. They emphasised that while semen confirmed

Exploring Forensics: Careers for Curious Minds: Pathways for Future Careers.

physical contact, it could not by itself prove whether the act was consensual or reconstruct the exact circumstances. They also noted the possibility of *secondary transfer* (DNA being moved indirectly), although it was considered unlikely in this case.

In court, the forensic biologist presented the results in plain, accessible language. They explained both the *strengths and the limitations* of DNA evidence. Because the evidence was presented clearly and without exaggeration, the jury understood its significance while appreciating its boundaries.

Exploring Forensics: Careers for Curious Minds: Pathways for Future Careers.

D. Word Search

Each puzzle contains important words from this chapter. They might be hidden forwards, backwards, up, down, or diagonally. Just like real investigations, you'll need to look carefully!

See if you can find all the words and challenge a friend to beat your time.

Exploring Forensics: Careers for Curious Minds: Pathways for Future Careers.

Forensic Biology Word Search

```
S Y C E P Q P L G Z B C Y I S A P C A M
H O X B Y P L Q N L T K T K D M S D U K
J G P E V I D E N C E G X H I H S T Q B
K Q X A Z E G M Z H H F I Q U L J A G O
B I O C H E M I S T R Y B C L X M R D X
V Y T V Y G U E H R B D M R F S I V K Y
Q R J N T S R K M M H H G A Y W B P S N
G Q T O I C Y V J I H P C T D F I D C O
N W Y I L I J U Q L R V B C O L H S G M
I M K T I T S E H H I X B K B A A Y A I
L M S A B S H W P N Z Q M F U N R D R T
I N S N A I U I H Q E U A N J O A L N S
F I J I B T N R X A B T H R T U K K X E
O W F M O A M Q L U J J C A V T T K R T
R U B A R T B Y S W A E R X X H E Z U A
P N C T P S N I V P Z O I X M K A R A F
A N B N X R D K H V B A G J E B S V R L
N E C O C K L L U A L V K G S A D H L D
D V A C T M W L L E X O N E R A T E H T
Z M F Q T G O M R V A G E D A N E S I A
```

- o DNA Profiling
- o Body Fluids
- o Evidence
- o Contamination
- o Statistics
- o Laboratory
- o Biochemisty
- o Probability
- o Testimony
- o Exonerate

Exploring Forensics: Careers for Curious Minds: Pathways for Future Careers.

Forensic Toxicology

A. Role Overview

Forensic toxicology is the science and practice of identifying drugs, poisons, and chemicals in biological material for legal purposes. Its central task is to establish whether substances contributed to injury or death, or if their presence gives insight into behaviour at the time of an incident. Toxicologists use sophisticated chemistry and pharmacology to answer questions central to matters of justice.

The analysis process begins with the selection of suitable biological matrices. Blood is the most direct indicator of the substances that were circulating at the time of death or offence, while urine may indicate past use over a longer period of time. Vitreous humour from the eye adds stability when other fluids have decomposed. Evidence of drug use may be gathered using the hair over many months, and where necessary, other tissues like liver or stomach contents may be investigated as well. There are strengths and weaknesses of each of the matrices, and the toxicologist should make a correct decision.

Exploring Forensics: Careers for Curious Minds: Pathways for Future Careers.

Method validation is basic. All the analytical methods, be they gas chromatography, liquid chromatography or mass spectrometry, should be shown to be reliable under specified conditions. Laboratories have stringent quality control measures, and this implies that the results will be repeatable and legally justifiable.

A special problem in post-mortem toxicology is redistribution. After death, drugs may migrate from one tissue to another and from one fluid to another, changing concentrations. Interpreting these results requires both scientific knowledge and awareness, as numbers alone can be misleading. Toxicologists, therefore, report not only the measured amounts but also their significance in death.

Reporting thresholds are thoroughly considered. The presence of a drug alone does not demonstrate impairment or fatality. Toxicologists state results in terms of concentrations, therapeutic ranges, and toxic levels, always taking into account the variability from person to person. The role requires clarity and balance in explaining results without overstatement. Ultimately, forensic toxicology is the means by which courts can have an informed assessment of the role of chemicals in life and death.

Exploring Forensics: Careers for Curious Minds: Pathways for Future Careers.

B. Pathways into the Role

In the United Kingdom, most forensic toxicologists typically begin with a degree in Chemistry, Biochemistry, or Toxicology. Some universities offer specialised courses in forensic science with an emphasis on analytical chemistry. Postgraduate training, whether at the Master's or doctoral level, may improve specialist training, but hands-on experience in the laboratory is crucial. Graduates are generally employed as analytical scientists in accredited forensic laboratories where they become competent under supervision.

Training consists of mastering complex instruments, sample preparation techniques, and stringent control of contamination. Work is closely associated with forensic pathologists, since toxicology tends to complement autopsy findings. Understanding the needs of coroners is especially important, as the results of toxicology are often the determining factor in whether a death is deemed natural, accidental or suspicious. The career advancement leads to the status of a reporting scientist, in which toxicologists interpret data, prepare formal reports, and give testimony in court. Networking and further development are supported by membership in professional organisations, such as the UK

Exploring Forensics: Careers for Curious Minds: Pathways for Future Careers.

and Ireland Association of Forensic Toxicologists (UKIAFT).

The opportunities for entry in the United States are generally similar; however, the emphasis on chemistry and pharmacology is particularly high at the undergraduate degree level. Bachelor's degrees in these subjects serve as the foundation for laboratory fellowships or entry-level positions. Many toxicologists go on to study further as postgraduates, acquiring specialisation in analytical methods. Training is conducted in laboratories that adhere to rigorous quality systems, ensuring validated methods and results that meet legal standards.

Certification routes give credence. The American Board of Forensic Toxicology (ABFT) provides certification to individuals and accreditation to laboratories. This credential is highly regarded and confirms that a toxicologist is compliant with recognised standards of competence.

Toxicologists in the US can work in a broad variety of settings. Post-mortem toxicology is the investigation to determine whether or not drugs or poisons contributed to death. In the case of drug-facilitated crime, such as sexual assault, toxicologists examine blood and urine for traces of incapacitating drugs. In the case of driving under the influence (DUI) cases, they test for alcohol and drugs to determine impairment. Each context requires that results be carefully interpreted and communicated.

Exposure to court is unavoidable in both the UK and the US. Toxicologists are required to write reports that explain scientific results in terms that are easy to understand and to testify under cross-examination. Multi-disciplinary working is prevalent, with toxicologists collaborating with pathologists, anthropologists, and police investigators. The career demands patience, precision and the capacity to handle scrutiny. For those who follow this path, forensic toxicology offers the potential to be both a skilled scientist and a direct servant of justice.

C. Case Study

A 45-year-old man was found dead at home. There were no signs of external injury, and police learned that he had a medical history including depression and high blood pressure, for which he took prescribed medication. An autopsy was ordered, and samples were submitted to the toxicology laboratory.

Exploring Forensics: Careers for Curious Minds: Pathways for Future Careers.

The forensic toxicologist began by designing an analytical strategy. Several body fluids were tested:

- *Blood*, which shows what substances were present in circulation at or near the time of death.
- *Urine*, which reflects drugs that the body has already processed and excreted.
- *Vitreous humour* (the fluid from inside the eye), which is chemically stable and helps confirm results even when blood may be degraded.

The first stage was *screening*, carried out using *immunoassay techniques*. These tests detect broad classes of drugs, such as opiates, benzodiazepines, or stimulants. Because they can sometimes give false positives, positive results are always confirmed.

The confirmation stage used *gas chromatography–mass spectrometry (GC–MS)*. This highly sensitive technique separates the chemical components and then identifies them by their unique "fingerprints" of mass and charge. This step not only confirms the drug's identity but also provides precise measurements of how much is present.

Exploring Forensics: Careers for Curious Minds: Pathways for Future Careers.

In this case, the results showed *therapeutic levels* of two prescription medications, meaning the concentrations were within the normal range expected for medical treatment. No alcohol or illicit drugs were detected.

The toxicologist interpreted these findings alongside the man's medical history. They explained that the drugs were unlikely to have directly caused death, although they were part of the overall health picture. The final medical conclusion was that the man's death was due to *natural disease*, with toxicology helping to rule out poisoning or overdose.

In the *coroner's court*, the toxicologist presented the results in plain terms. They emphasised that:

- The presence of a drug does *not* automatically mean it caused harm.
- Drug concentrations must always be considered in the context of medical history and other autopsy findings.

By explaining both the strengths and the limitations of the data, the toxicologist ensured the court understood the evidence clearly and avoided misleading assumptions.

Exploring Forensics: Careers for Curious Minds: Pathways for Future Careers.

D. Word Search

Each puzzle contains important words from this chapter. They might be hidden forwards, backwards, up, down, or diagonally. Just like real investigations, you'll need to look carefully!

See if you can find all the words and challenge a friend to beat your time.

Exploring Forensics: Careers for Curious Minds: Pathways for Future Careers.

Forensic Toxicology Word Search

```
C N R E D I S T R I B U T I O N B Z X I
J Z G A V L K V H X O Q W B R L B Q H I
S M V I T R E O U S H U M O U R R G W X
I I M M U N O A S S A Y W H H B X H X S
F E C H R O M A T O G R A P H Y G L M J
F E R I G T K X Z D Y I Z T T T M J Y U
X G L X Y C O N C E N T R A T I O N S E
O Z N K K Z R Z P H A R M A C O L O G Y
K F X P A U Z C B I O C H E M I S T R Y
Q E F Q R Q L Y F S B K F E S L A J U I
H Q W H N N B G Q N S I U H N Z K M Q B
W A P D A U E O J O O L G I A X P O Y T
X G F K U U M L T S G G Q Z E P A N A I
I S C X A Q Y O V I D J Y M I V C S X E
D H N E C A M C M O I P B J O S N X Y I
Y B H R Y D I I D P S X Q S U U X Y N Z
A K D L D Z D X L C J Q T C D E R B T K
B V N F Q X V O E H X D F O D N K X Q X
X U X N T V A T N F Q R C T U I G Z O U
D J K S L A B O R A T O R Y Q C I B Y S
```

- o Toxicology
- o Chromatography
- o Biochemistry
- o Laboratory
- o Poisons
- o Pharmacology
- o Redistribution
- o Vitreous Humour
- o Concentrations
- o Immunoassay

Exploring Forensics: Careers for Curious Minds: Pathways for Future Careers.

Forensic Nursing (Sexual Offence and Clinical Roles)

CAUTION: MENTION OF SEXUAL ASSAULT

A. Role Overview

Forensic nursing is at the crossroads of care and justice. The first duty of the nurse is to the patient, but the service also needs to maintain evidence to a standard that the courts can have confidence in. Post-assault survivors need calm, privacy and clear choices. A trauma-informed approach offers all three. It explains what is going to happen, seeks consent step by step, and gives the survivor control over the pace and detail.

Extensive documentation is made linking the clinical and forensic aims. Injuries are documented using measurements, anatomical diagrams, and photographs, where consent is obtained. Notes describe the story in neutral language, separating the patient's words from the examiner's. When evidence is required, sampling is done on agreed protocols. Swabs, combings, toxicology tubes, and clothing are handled using clean technique, labelled immediately, sealed, and logged so that continuity is never an issue.

Exploring Forensics: Careers for Curious Minds: Pathways for Future Careers.

Safeguarding is a component of each and every decision. Risk is evaluated, from acute safety to the potential of intimidation or self-harm. The nurse outlines options for medical treatment, counselling and police contact, and honours the choice made. When children or vulnerable adults are involved, statutory duties provide guidance on the sharing and protection of information.

In the United Kingdom, a large number of services are run through Sexual Assault Referral Centres. These enable healthcare and capture of evidence without the pressure of having to file a police report, allowing time to consider the next step. Working across various settings, the nurse serves as both an advocate and an impartial professional, providing support, accuracy, and care in their approach, ensuring that their statements align with the evidence.

B. Pathways into the Role

The path in the United Kingdom begins with registration as a nurse through an approved degree and admission to the Nursing and Midwifery Council. Experience in emergency, sexual health, paediatrics, or community services would be beneficial and can assist in developing confidence in acute

Exploring Forensics: Careers for Curious Minds: Pathways for Future Careers.

assessment and sensitive discussions. Subsequently, nurses receive training in the examination of forensic or sexual offences by NHS providers or professional bodies.

Training is a combination of classroom teaching and supervised practice. Under mentorship, trainees learn evidence recovery, interpretation of injuries, toxicology sampling, taking photos, and note-taking that will be presented in court, among other subjects. They also practise giving clear explanations to patients as well as writing statements that can be understood by a jury. Inter-agency working is central, with the role having links to police, safeguarding teams, social care, laboratories, and independent advocacy. Competence is maintained through ongoing professional development, peer review, and regular updates in trauma care, consent, and law.

In the United States, nurses become Registered Nurses, and then pursue specialist training and credentials as Sexual Assault Nurse Examiners for adults or for paediatrics. Programmes established didactic hours, clinical simulation, and observed exams. Services anticipate a collection of cases, reflective logs, and ongoing supervision prior to independent practice. SANEs work in hospitals, crisis centres and community clinics, and work closely with advocacy services and law enforcement while keeping the patient's autonomy at the centre.

Across both systems, success depends on three strands that are held together: strong clinical skills, disciplined forensic practice, and humane communication. The work is demanding. This requires the ability to remain calm under pressure, have a sense of ethics when making complex decisions, and resilience in the face of upsetting material. The reward is tangible: safer patients, better evidence and a fairer process.

C. Case Study

Late one evening, an adult survivor came to a *Sexual Assault Referral Centre (SARC)*. A forensic nurse welcomed her, assessed her immediate safety, and explained the available options: medical treatment, evidence collection, counselling, and the choice to speak with the police either immediately or at a later stage. *Consent* was obtained step by step, allowing time for questions and the option to decline any part of the process.

Exploring Forensics: Careers for Curious Minds: Pathways for Future Careers.

The nurse followed a *structured plan of care*. First came a history and risk assessment, focusing on the survivor's health and safety. With consent, any injuries were documented in notes and photographs. Swabs were taken from agreed-upon areas, *toxicology samples* were collected within the recommended timeframes, and clothing was dried, packaged, sealed, and logged to ensure forensic integrity. Throughout the exam, the nurse provided clear warnings before each procedure, paused whenever requested, and confirmed that the patient could stop at any time.

Before discharge, the nurse provided *emergency contraception* and medication to reduce the risk of infection *(prophylaxis)* and made referrals for follow-up tests. A *safety plan* was made, which included secure accommodation, support contacts, and instructions for returning if symptoms changed. All evidence and paperwork were stored securely, following *chain of custody rules*, so the material would remain admissible if the survivor chose to pursue a case later.

Weeks afterwards, the survivor decided to report the assault. The evidence was transferred to the forensic laboratory, and the nurse wrote a clear statement, carefully separating

Exploring Forensics: Careers for Curious Minds: Pathways for Future Careers.

factual observations (what was seen and done) from interpretation. In court, the nurse explained the process in everyday language and stayed within professional limits, presenting evidence without drawing unsupported conclusions.

Exploring Forensics: Careers for Curious Minds: Pathways for Future Careers.

D. Word Search

Each puzzle contains important words from this chapter. They might be hidden forwards, backwards, up, down, or diagonally. Just like real investigations, you'll need to look carefully!

See if you can find all the words and challenge a friend to beat your time.

Exploring Forensics: Careers for Curious Minds: Pathways for Future Careers.

Forensic Nursing Word Search

```
R J Y V Y K S A F E G U A R D I N G R J
I Z L D H I Y G Q Z R T C Z V J V X X E
R H F J T F H E B U F F B H Z B V U M R
K T B B X Q J T O Z D U B I F E H G D O
Q C R C O N S E N T O T Y J U S H N G P
M L Q A U Y W W M Z T T J T R Z H I P I
G E Y S S M I N T E G R I T Y M J S V B
T Y R P K V M N U O L B P B I M T R F X
P B E W M E L O Q T W R W O C X N U V Q
V Z V T E X Y I Y M O O O Z X V E N F J
U C O E P X J T P E S A O S K E M C E J
N U C Y S R C A O E Q H T N D X E I N C
W O E Q T J U T G C A B T M P O T S Z L
R F R B Q J P N V N A W I L Y B A N C O
Q A K R N R E E U E K X S P Q Z T E W S
O F N R H O D M A D V O C A C Y S R K G
A T V V B J C U D I S D X P C Z H O C B
O D Q T M D H C A V V C M R H I E F N I
T T R A U M A O I E C Y T T B Y Z V C B
K V Q D P F W D L X D F U D P J F O M K
```

- o Forensic Nursing
- o Documentation
- o Evidence
- o Safeguarding
- o Consent
- o Advocacy
- o Trauma
- o Integrity
- o Statement
- o Recovery

Forensic Odontology

A. Role Overview

Forensic odontology is the application of the science of dentistry to questions of the law. The unique features of teeth and jaws can assist in their identification and analysis. The most recognised task is dental identification of deceased persons in situations when fingerprints or DNA are unavailable or degraded. Teeth are tough, surviving fire, immersion and decomposition, making them invaluable in both individual cases and large-scale disasters.

The process starts with a detailed charting of all the teeth and the restorations. Forensic odontologists match these findings from post-mortem comparisons with those from antemortem dental records and radiographs provided by family dentists or health authorities. Even minute details, such as root morphology, pattern of fillings, or crown shape, can prove identity to a high degree of certainty.

Bite mark assessment is another field of practice, but is done with more caution. Patterns left on skin or objects might help match a suspect with an assault, but research has revealed that bite marks can distort, and that interpretation is prone to bias. Modern practitioners therefore place great emphasis on careful documentation and the use of high-resolution photography, and being able to clearly communicate limitations when presenting such evidence in court.

Disaster victim identification (DVI) often beckons odontologists to the field. Following earthquakes, air crashes, or mass-casualty fires, they work in a multidisciplinary team, collecting and interpreting dental evidence using the Interpol DVI protocol. Quality assurance is very important throughout. Peer review, double charting and regular calibration provide protection against error and unconscious bias.

The work requires both clinical precision and emotional resiliency. Odontologists must work in difficult settings; temporary mortuaries, remote locations or the sites of catastrophic loss without compromising accuracy and dignity to the deceased or their families.

B. Pathways into the Role

Entry into the profession in the United Kingdom is through a recognised dental degree and registration with the General

Exploring Forensics: Careers for Curious Minds: Pathways for Future Careers.

Dental Council. After establishing competence in general dentistry, practitioners can pursue postgraduate training in forensic odontology, which is offered through universities and professional organisations. These programmes include dental identification, radiographic interpretation, disaster protocols and expert witness skills.

Practical experience is a necessity. Some trainees volunteer in the identification teams in the region or serve in the mortuaries under supervision, gaining experience with the charting, photographing, and handling of evidence processes. Membership of the British Association of Forensic Odontology (BAFO), which provides membership, mentoring, peer review and continuing education. Regular calibration exercises are conducted, ensuring that practitioners can rely on consistent standards when comparing dental records.

In the United States, dentists follow a similar course. After receiving a Doctor of Dental Surgery (DDS) or Doctor of Dental Medicine (DMD) degree and licensure by the state, they can then pursue specialist courses or fellowships in forensic odontology. Programmes recognised by the American Board of Forensic Odontology (ABFO) are a combination of academic study and practical casework.

Exploring Forensics: Careers for Curious Minds: Pathways for Future Careers.

Certification by the ABFO is highly respected and requires documentation of identification, bite mark, and courtroom experience.

Both UK and US practitioners are being encouraged to join disaster response rosters so that they can be mobilised in the event of major incidents. Training exercises with law enforcement, emergency services and international DVI teams develop the skills to work efficiently under pressure. Continuous professional development is mandatory. New imaging technologies, improvements in the integration of DNA, and changing legal standards mean there is a constant need for updates.

The role is not limited to technical skills. Forensic odontologists must compose concise, impartial reports and present findings in a manner that is comprehensible to coroners, medical examiners, and the courts. They collaborate with pathologists, anthropologists, and all other forensic professionals to ensure that dental evidence is used to support the overall work in the investigation. The route is challenging, and it is a rare combination of clinical expertise, humanitarian labour, and direct involvement in justice that it affords.

Exploring Forensics: Careers for Curious Minds: Pathways for Future Careers.

C. Case Study

After a massive air disaster, an international *Disaster Victim Identification (DVI)* team was deployed. Among the specialists were forensic odontologists, whose role was to confirm the identities of the deceased. Temporary mortuaries were established near the crash site, equipped for systematic examinations.

The dental team first collected *antemortem records* from families, dentists, and national health services. These included dental charts, treatment notes, and radiographs (X-rays). All records were catalogued and digitised for rapid comparison.

During *post-mortem examinations*, odontologists cleaned and charted jaws and teeth, recording restorations, missing teeth, and distinctive features. Radiographs were taken to match root and sinus patterns to antemortem files. In one notable case, a victim's *dentures carried a serial number* engraved by the manufacturer. This number was traced back to a dentist who had supplied them, providing a positive identification even where other methods had failed.

Exploring Forensics: Careers for Curious Minds: Pathways for Future Careers.

To ensure accuracy, each identification was double-checked by a second examiner. This rigorous process confirmed the identities of many victims when fingerprints and visual recognition were no longer possible due to fire and trauma.

The dental reports were presented to the DVI commission, which informed families and enabled the return of remains for burial.

D. Word Search

Each puzzle contains important words from this chapter. They might be hidden forwards, backwards, up, down, or diagonally. Just like real investigations, you'll need to look carefully!

See if you can find all the words and challenge a friend to beat your time.

Exploring Forensics: Careers for Curious Minds: Pathways for Future Careers.

Forensic Odontology Word Search

```
F O R E N S I C O D O N T O L O G Y A B
G G L Y O P B K K L D N T O L J L S I V
C H K B N V R E S T O R A T I O N S Z Y
B Y N K M E K M R A D I O G R A P H S M
J U G D A A J I R T E R W J L J M B A T
R S Z B W G I R S R N A G I D L G L T L
P B D E U W V K X L V U I L U Q K R L O
B Y T O S O L V F Q D L W H O B V Q F C
K Z U Q J T E B J Q J B G Z G N Z J A O
R E S I L I E N C Y L W O M G O C M B T
I D E N T I F I C A T I O N O B T R R O
O M G X U M A H O B I T E M A R K S B R
I S D C B P H E J G R P E V B Z U D E P
F V J C H A R T I N G H W M Y V K Z O X
N G D I S A S T E R V I C T I M C O Q D
N V C G P E X H C S H T E E T H U T B W
X F A Y T I Q R W I C U I J C U I B V V
A M X J X P V P V S M F M E U R H B G F
X R Y W Y Y Q W T O L Q Q Y W P V Z M I
P Q I Y U Z Y D C V G K R K M W N F O V
```

- Forensic
- Odontology
- Identification
- Bite Marks
- Radiographs
- Charting
- Disaster Victim
- Teeth
- Restorations
- Protocol
- Resilience

Exploring Forensics: Careers for Curious Minds: Pathways for Future Careers.

Forensic Psychology

A. Role Overview

Forensic psychology is the application of the science of human behaviour to questions of law. Practitioners help assess offenders and advise courts, as well as assist agencies in understanding the psychological factors that affect crime and justice. Their work ranges from prisons, hospitals, probation services and courtrooms and involves both clinical ability and a solid application of scientific reasoning.

One important job is to assess offenders. Psychologists evaluate mental condition, likelihood of recidivism, and the capacity of individuals to engage in legal processes. They use systematic tools and tried-and-true interview techniques to look for risk factors like impulsivity, a history of violence, or drug or alcohol abuse. These tests are used to help determine sentences, treatment plans, and when to release someone.

Fitness to plead and competence are also very important. A forensic psychologist may determine if a defendant possesses the capability to comprehend the charges, instruct legal counsel, and adhere to court procedures. Their results

Exploring Forensics: Careers for Curious Minds: Pathways for Future Careers.

can determine whether a trial should proceed or if additional steps are necessary.

A significant portion of the work is based on how effectively you can conduct interviews with people. In many cases, psychologists speak with suspects, witnesses, and victims when they are under considerable stress. They must remain impartial by establishing rapport without directing or swaying any testimony. Research on eyewitness memory has implications for their practice, assisting their role in evaluating the reliability of identification evidence in court.

Forensic psychologists are often called as expert witnesses. They write lengthy reports and provide testimony, breaking down complex psychological concepts into language that judges and juries can understand. They always follow strict ethical rules, such as maintaining confidentiality, avoiding dual relationships, and not succumbing to pressure to draw conclusions that aren't supported by the evidence. Their job requires them to be very accurate, independent, and aware of the impact their work has on others.

Exploring Forensics: Careers for Curious Minds: Pathways for Future Careers.

B. Pathways into the Role

In the UK, the first step is to obtain a psychology degree recognised by the British Psychological Society. After that, graduates must complete postgraduate training and a period of supervised practice, typically through a Doctorate in Forensic Psychology or a Stage Two BPS qualification. This supervised stage gives you experience in prisons, secure hospitals, probation services, and community programs. Candidates compile a portfolio of tests, treatment plans, and research projects to demonstrate their qualifications.

Psychologists who pass the assessment become practitioner psychologists and register with the Health and Care Professions Council. Many people keep learning by going to specialised workshops on topics like sexual offending, assessing the risk of violence, and trauma. People typically begin gaining courtroom experience by writing reports and then progress to giving oral testimony.

In the United States, a bachelor's degree in psychology or a related field is required, followed by a doctoral degree (PhD or PsyD) in clinical or forensic psychology. You need to complete supervised clinical hours, which typically involve working in correctional facilities, forensic hospitals, or court clinics. States then issue licenses to candidates, which

Exploring Forensics: Careers for Curious Minds: Pathways for Future Careers.

require them to pass tests and demonstrate proof of supervised practice.

Forensic psychologists can work in prisons, mental health services, or private practice in both the public and private sectors. Many of them divide their time between conducting assessments, providing therapy, and engaging in research. They need to stay up to date on laws, rules for psychological testing, and ethical codes. Joining professional groups like the BPS Division of Forensic Psychology or the American Psychological Association's Division 41 will help you keep learning and get your work reviewed by others.

Success in the field doesn't just depend on doing well in school. Practitioners need to be able to handle challenging situations, such as violent crime and child protection cases. In this job, they need to be able to explain their findings to people who aren't experts in the field while still maintaining scientific accuracy. Most importantly, they must remain neutral and ensure that their opinions are beneficial to the court, not just one side of the case.

**Exploring Forensics: Careers for Curious Minds:
Pathways for Future Careers.**

C. Case Study

A middle-aged defendant was charged with serious assault. Because of his history of mental illness and recent hospital admissions, the defence questioned whether he was *fit to plead*, that is, able to take part fairly in his trial. The court ordered a forensic psychological examination.

The psychologist began by reviewing *medical records and psychiatric reports*, and then conducted *structured clinical interviews*. Standardised tools were also used, such as the *MacArthur Competence Assessment Tool – Criminal Adjudication (MacCAT-CA)*, which evaluates whether someone understands legal proceedings, can communicate with their lawyer, and can follow a trial.

The assessment focused on three main areas:

1. Understanding the charges and possible outcomes.
2. Ability to give instructions to a solicitor.
3. Ability to follow the trial process.

Testing showed the defendant had *moderate cognitive impairment* but still had a reasonable understanding of proceedings. He could correctly explain the roles of the

Exploring Forensics: Careers for Curious Minds: Pathways for Future Careers.

judge, jury, and lawyers, and knew what penalties could result from conviction. However, his attention span was limited, and he struggled to comprehend complex information when it was presented in detail. The psychologist recommended *accommodations,* such as more frequent breaks during hearings and providing simplified written summaries of evidence.

In a *detailed report to the court*, the psychologist described the methods used, the results obtained, and the limits of interpretation. They also emphasised that competence can *fluctuate over time*, meaning ongoing monitoring would be important. When testifying, the psychologist avoided jargon and presented the findings neutrally, highlighting both strengths and weaknesses rather than advocating for either side.

The judge accepted the opinion and ruled that the defendant was fit to plead, provided reasonable adjustments were made.

Exploring Forensics: Careers for Curious Minds: Pathways for Future Careers.

D. Word Search

Each puzzle contains important words from this chapter. They might be hidden forwards, backwards, up, down, or diagonally. Just like real investigations, you'll need to look carefully!

See if you can find all the words and challenge a friend to beat your time.

Exploring Forensics: Careers for Curious Minds: Pathways for Future Careers.

Forensic Psychology Word Search

```
Y J H Z W B T W E S N N O Y X W Z U B Q
D S R Y P I K E Y F W U T Z A I E N Z G
M U U S D W R I G S N I D Y D B K F C H
S A J C J O T V O T F O L X N D A P K R
I A R I Y J E R L T P M D H N M U Q N W
V Q B H T C F E O C X U W J X F T E N N
I J X T I V N T H W U G I V U S T U V Y
D R P E L Y F N C L Q B D F F T K Y R Y
I T G C A O Z I Y E R P N J Z W X O A K
C N T X I M W R S C Y A V J Y P M J T S
E E J N T Q L F P N N C K Q S E G E K B
R M X D N B M H C E O C G B M R W L L O
D S Q B E R N X I T M X K F I Y W X Y X
B S S H D W K S S E I U T L M E X O Y V
X E V P I Q X V N P T X R P D P B V O S
Z S R C F Q E E E M S W G M G I S P K T
C S K T N Z A D R O E S E Q T C N Y O A
Z A V J O K R V O C T L T V J N Y D J W
A P B S C C B Z F T F C X H A W K I X R
H M S K K L M E Y E W I T N E S S W B Y
```

- Forensic Psychology
- Assessment
- Interview
- Recidivism
- Competence
- Eyewitness
- Memory
- Confidentiality
- Ethics
- Testimony

Exploring Forensics: Careers for Curious Minds: Pathways for Future Careers.

Forensic Accounting

A. Role Overview

Forensic accounting is a process of tracing the money to respond to legal questions. Practitioners review records, reconstruct transactions and implement financial behaviour in a manner that can be trusted by the courts and regulators. The work encompasses a range of activities, from civil disputes to regulatory inquiries and criminal prosecutions. It requires technical knowledge of accounting standards, keen investigative judgment, and the ability to communicate the complex findings of the investigation to others in simple language.

Fraud examination is at the centre of the role. Forensic accountants investigate various schemes, including false invoicing, payroll fraud, kickbacks, asset misappropriation, and financial statement manipulation. They evaluate control environments, charting out processes and identifying where duties have malfunctioned or overlap. Red flags can manifest themselves in unusual journal entries, round-sum payments, supplier clustering or sudden margin changes.

Exploring Forensics: Careers for Curious Minds: Pathways for Future Careers.

Data analytics serves to magnify these enquiries. Using general ledger extracts, bank statements, purchasing data, emails, and device logs, analysts run tests to identify duplicates, anomalies, and patterns over time. Benford's law, ratio analysis, link analysis, and period-end cut-off testing help expose hidden risks. E-discovery tools facilitate targeted searches of communications, and visual dashboards aid in understanding the flows between entities and accounts.

Interviews provide context to the numbers. Preparatory planning defines objectives, roles and disclosure obligations. Interviews are structured, unbiased and recorded. The goal is to test hypotheses, though, not to trap witnesses. Notes differentiate between what's fact and what's opinion and keep track of any admissions or contradictions. Where appropriate, findings are cross-checked against independent evidence to avoid confirmation bias.

Reporting knits the strands together. In civil matters, there are reports of claims of breach of contract, misrepresentation or loss of business interruption. In criminal cases, they help the police and prosecutors by quantifying loss and tracing the proceeds of crime. Disclosure duties are of the utmost importance. Workpapers, data sources, and assumptions must be made available for inspection. Where expert evidence is provided, opinions are restricted to the area of the expert's experience, methodologies are explained, and uncertainties are indicated.

Throughout, objectivity is non-negotiable. Forensic accountants need to maintain a clear chain of custody to records, strictly observe the boundaries of legal privilege, and separate their own opinions from evidence. The craft is in being able to take messy data and turn it into defensible findings, without being neutral, transparent and proportionate.

B. Pathways into the Role

In the United Kingdom, most practitioners are qualified through the ACA, ACCA, or CIMA routes, and often start out in audit, where they are introduced to controls testing, sampling, and documentation. Exposure to investigations occurs through internal audit, risk or specialist forensic teams within professional services firms and industry. Specialist fraud training, including interviewing, e-discovery basics and analytics tools, builds capability. Memberships and short courses with recognised bodies help

Exploring Forensics: Careers for Curious Minds: Pathways for Future Careers.

to enhance credibility and contribute towards continuing professional development. Career paths include practice (advisory firms), in-house investigative bodies, regulatory agencies, or support for law enforcement. Senior positions include leading multidisciplinary teams, providing expert evidence, and disclosing such evidence in litigation or arbitration.

In the United States, the standard entry route is through a CPA, with early career experience in audit or advisory services. Many practitioners include specialist qualifications in fraud investigation or valuation to demonstrate their competence in the areas of disputes and investigations. Experience is gained in issues such as revenue recognition, procurement irregularities, healthcare claims, and Foreign Corrupt Practices Act (FCPA) risk. Litigation support work involves drafting reports, developing discovery protocols, preparing depositions, and collaborating with counsel. E-discovery literacy is becoming an increasingly expected requirement, including preservation warnings, custodian interviews, effective use of search term design, and awareness of metadata.

Across these two jurisdictions, the transition from analyst to expert relies on judgment, independence, and communication. Analysts learn to scope work in proportion, keep workpapers defensible and how to write a report that a non-accountant could follow. Experts perfect courtroom skills, handling cross-examination and explaining methods without advocacy. The best practitioners have a combination of technical accuracy and restraint, stating what the evidence shows, what it does not show, and what other plausible explanations are.

C. Case Study

A local authority noticed that one of its facilities contracts was costing far more than expected. To investigate, they brought in forensic accountants, specialists who apply financial investigation techniques to uncover fraud.

The accountants began by analysing two years of transactions linked to the contract. Right away, they noticed several *red flags*:

- Many purchase orders were just under the limit that required extra approval.
- Several invoices were approved late at night or on weekends, often by the same manager.

Exploring Forensics: Careers for Curious Minds: Pathways for Future Careers.

- Some newly created vendors appeared to share the *same bank details* as existing companies.

Using *data analytics*, the team tested the records for unusual patterns. They looked for duplicate invoices, sequential invoice numbers across supposedly different vendors, and round-number payments that didn't match any work records. Contract rules required competitive quotes for high-value jobs; however, in many cases, exceptions were logged without explanation.

Interviews were then carried out. First, process owners explained how the procurement cycle was supposed to work. Then the approving manager was questioned. During the interview, investigators compared his answers with email trails, security logs, and accounting records. They also discovered that background checks on new vendors had sometimes been skipped when jobs were marked as "urgent."

The final report identified suspicious payments, potential *kickbacks*, and weaknesses in internal controls. It recommended:

- Halting payments to suspect vendors.

Exploring Forensics: Careers for Curious Minds: Pathways for Future Careers.

- Seeking restitution and insurance recovery.
- Reporting the case to law enforcement.
- Introducing stronger controls, such as stricter approval rules, vendor due diligence, and regular data analytics.

The authority followed the plan. Some funds were recovered, fraudulent vendors were removed, and new systems were put in place to prevent the same scheme from happening again.

Exploring Forensics: Careers for Curious Minds: Pathways for Future Careers.

D. Word Search

Each puzzle contains important words from this chapter. They might be hidden forwards, backwards, up, down, or diagonally. Just like real investigations, you'll need to look carefully!

See if you can find all the words and challenge a friend to beat your time.

Exploring Forensics: Careers for Curious Minds: Pathways for Future Careers.

Forensic Accounting Word Search

```
L H O C U X Y B O U U G V F D K W I Q V
Z O O S Q C O N T R O L S L D I N C C W
L D A T A A N A L Y T I C S N X H B Y P
R Q S Y W H V A R P R Q N F G N Q Q D X
J F N W I H E L X J Y P Q N W T H Z G Y
S F A W M P X S Z Z Z I S U P O P W C
K W D S B S A D Q B M T B E O J S A C N
F S D B Z N Z P U P R S C Q G W M I S E
R Q Y V I S S C C O L N F S E K V Y P R
J Q D F N M W G P V E N N I K Y G D W A
C B S H H A G E H D S O V Y I T H U C P
M R X T X W R J I D I R M S W I N A O S
G D A D C Q E V H T E J J D V V F R P N
X S M S N A E M C T X D I I C I H F Y A
A U D I T E S A N V Z D A F G T H W S R
V K Z M G W S I E M H D R X T C B L H T
T A Q Y Y N B A F J F C U M D E H F Z Y
O M L I A X O O C H V B E B P J U P M X
H P X R V P E J N O H L L P M B N K E H
L N T C H P Y H O T X S M D I O C E A E
```

- Audit
- Fraud
- Transactions
- Data Analytics
- Interviews
- Objectivity
- Evidence
- Controls
- Reporting
- Transparency

Exploring Forensics: Careers for Curious Minds: Pathways for Future Careers.

Detective Work (Investigative Pathway)

A. Role Overview

Information is transformed into evidence through detective work. It begins with a plan. Investigators define the incident, establish objectives and determine what needs to be prioritised in the first few hours. They make hypotheses and check them against the facts. Clear planning avoids wasted effort and ensures the enquiry is proportionate to the risk and harm.

At the centre of the craft are interviews. Detectives take preliminary accounts and then conduct structured interviews with witnesses and suspects. They prepare meticulously, selecting an approach that is open, fair and lawful. Good interviewing takes patience, active listening and accurate note-taking. It avoids contamination of memory and records what is said and what is not said.

Intelligence development is parallel to interviews. Detectives utilise local knowledge, patterns of crime, and analytical tools. They request that databases be searched and reviewed for prior incidents that share common features, such as location, method, or time. Open-source material, community reports and confidential sources enter the picture. The aim is to go from signals to leads and from leads to lines of enquiry, which can be tested.

Partnership with forensic units is routine. Detectives confer with scene investigators to determine priorities for the investigation, agree on sampling strategies, and track exhibits from recovery to the lab. They know what DNA, fingerprints, footwear marks or phone downloads can and cannot prove. This is to prevent overreach and to help provide realistic expectations for the case.

Disclosure obligations influence each step. Material that might help the defence or discredit the prosecution needs to be identified, recorded and disclosed as required under law. Case files must have structure, chronology and audit trails to enable decisions to be reviewed. Detectives work closely with prosecutors and present evidence that can be relied upon and understood.

Community impact is always taken into account. A crime series can provoke fear and disruption to people's daily lives. Detectives plan reassurance activity, communicate key messages through neighbourhood teams and listen to concerns. Success is not measured solely by the number of arrests, but also by the confidence of the public in the consequences of crime.

B. Pathways into the Role

In the United Kingdom, most detectives begin their careers as police constables. Entry is available through either the Police Constable Degree Apprenticeship or the Degree Holder Entry Programme. Early service develops the key skills in responding to, protecting, and handling evidence. Candidates then enter into a detective pathway. This incorporates structured learning, supervised casework, interview technique, file preparation and disclosure practice assessment. Professional development then continues with courses in serious crime, cyber investigations and public protection. Safeguarding training is key. Detectives learn to manage risk to victims and witnesses and to liaise with social care and health services.

In the United States, recruits attend a police academy and then work in patrol to obtain practical experience. Promotion to detective is by excellent performance and competitive selection. Many departments have specialist squads such as robbery, homicide, family violence, cybercrime and financial crime. Detectives are trained in interview techniques, search and seizure laws, digital evidence and case file management. Collaboration with prosecutors is part of day-to-day work. Joint case conferences match up the steps in the investigation with the rules of evidence and the needs of trial preparation.

Across both systems, the role rewards curiosity, discipline, and integrity. Detectives must be able to write comprehensible reports, work shifts and call-outs, and remain level-headed in high-risk situations. They learn to manage multi-agency enquiries, brief senior leaders, and give testimony with precision. Career progression involves responsibility for strategy, as well as the leadership of teams. The best detectives never stop learning, are adaptable to new kinds of crime, and continue to maintain the trust of the public by consistently doing the basics well.

C. Case Study

A series of evening robberies was reported near local transport hubs. Detectives quickly set priorities: to protect the public, preserve each crime scene, and identify the responsible party.

Exploring Forensics: Careers for Curious Minds: Pathways for Future Careers.

Patrol officers increased their presence in the area during peak times, while detectives began reviewing *CCTV footage* and past crime reports. From the CCTV, investigators noticed a person wearing a *distinctive jacket* and walking with a recognisable gait at several different locations.

Next, detectives worked with telecoms specialists to analyse *cell site data* (signals from mobile phones connecting to nearby towers). One phone number kept appearing in the same locations and at the same times as the robberies. With legal authority, subscriber information was obtained, narrowing down a potential suspect.

Witness interviews were conducted in a structured way. First, witnesses gave free recall statements in their own words. Later, detectives asked focused questions about specific details such as the suspect's clothing and behaviour.

A suspect soon emerged who matched the description and had a history of street robbery. Search warrants were issued, leading to the recovery of the distinctive jacket and a phone linked to the incriminating cell site records.

During interrogation, the suspect gave statements that conflicted with *travel card data* and CCTV timelines.

Exploring Forensics: Careers for Curious Minds: Pathways for Future Careers.

Forensic examination of the jacket also revealed *fibres from a victim's bag*, linking him directly to one of the robberies.

The final case file presented to prosecutors included:

- A timeline of all incidents.
- CCTV footage and telecoms records.
- Witness interviews.
- Forensic results.
- A full exhibit and disclosure list.

The evidence provided a clear picture of events. The suspect was charged, and the robberies stopped. Community updates later explained how *teamwork between patrols, detectives, forensics, telecoms,* and *witnesses* led to solving the case.

Answers to Word Searches

Well done for completing the word searches. They were designed to reinforce the key points discussed in each chapter. Now, let's see if you got any correct.

Exploring Forensics: Careers for Curious Minds: Pathways for Future Careers.

Forensic Anthropology

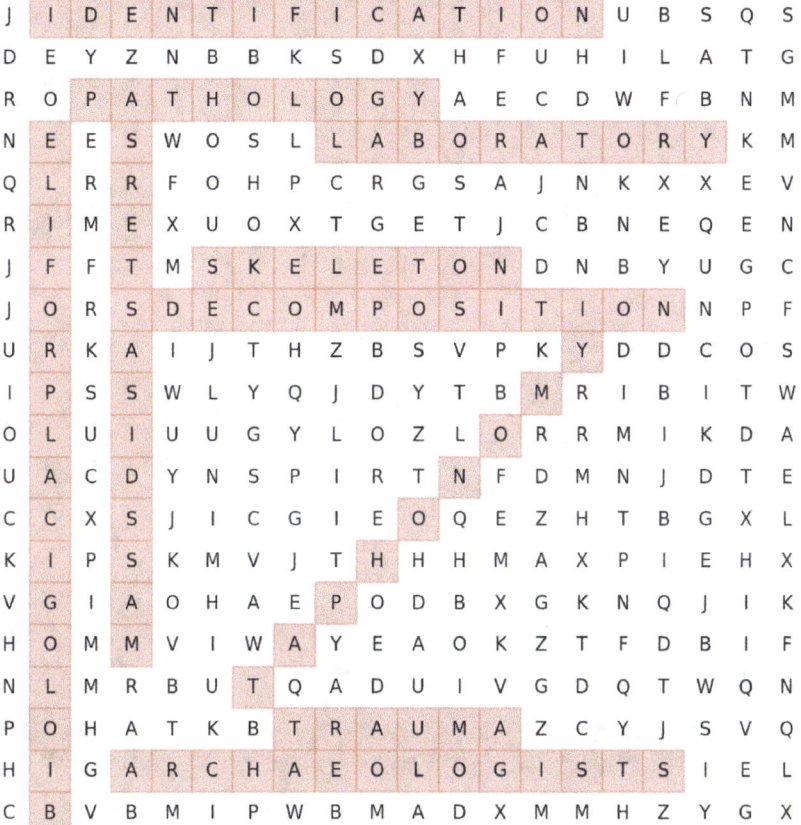

Exploring Forensics: Careers for Curious Minds: Pathways for Future Careers.

Forensic Pathology

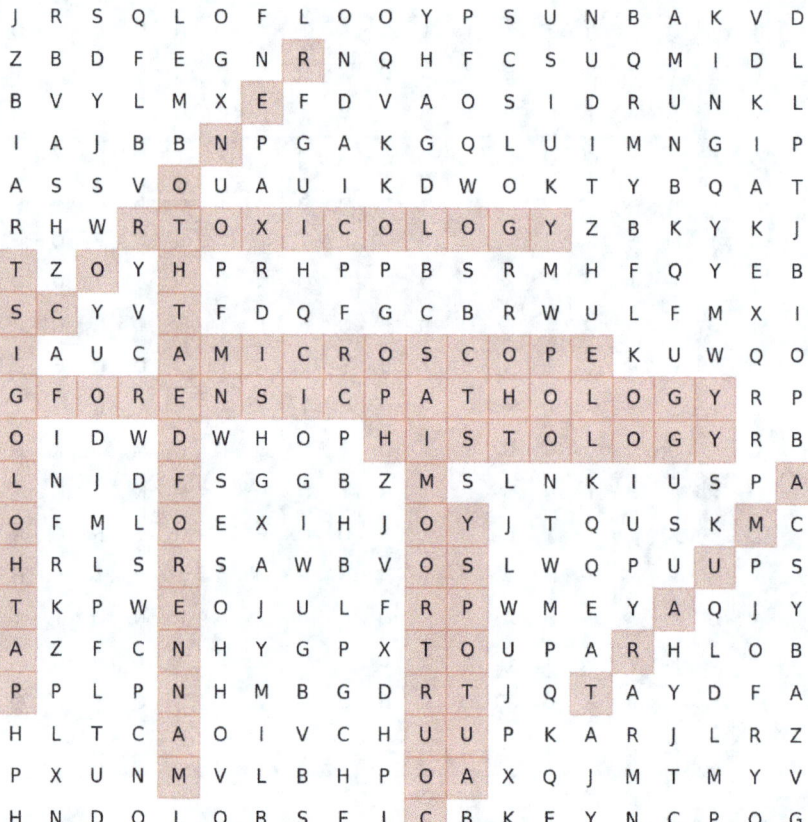

Exploring Forensics: Careers for Curious Minds: Pathways for Future Careers.

Crime Scene Investigation (CSI/SOCO)

K	R	T	E	S	T	I	M	O	N	Y	L	G	O	N	J	O	T	G	H
B	L	O	O	D	S	P	L	A	T	T	E	R	O	U	C	Q	Q	Y	K
A	P	K	H	R	R	Z	W	G	X	I	E	I	I	X	N	S	Y	V	P
O	W	X	D	J	S	V	W	L	E	V	T	I	Y	S	A	J	A	X	G
I	F	H	T	W	L	M	V	T	X	A	C	B	R	D	X	Z	W	Z	E
L	U	Z	J	N	V	I	H	S	T	V	D	O	E	G	X	B	S	K	X
M	Q	U	Z	X	F	C	K	N	B	E	T	M	D	V	O	M	S	Y	Y
S	E	L	K	W	U	R	E	N	T	A	Y	E	V	O	O	S	U	J	U
W	C	U	N	F	H	M	Y	V	G	H	I	F	K	M	R	O	T	R	N
E	N	G	A	T	U	Q	U	I	P	R	Q	E	O	Y	Z	M	E	J	W
Y	E	Q	M	C	K	L	T	A	Q	T	H	G	G	X	X	Z	V	G	P
M	D	B	O	E	R	S	R	G	V	Z	J	B	A	R	H	V	M	U	F
B	I	D	G	J	E	G	C	V	A	W	G	B	W	D	S	G	P	H	A
F	V	F	X	V	O	B	F	I	N	G	E	R	P	R	I	N	T	S	I
N	E	J	N	T	O	F	M	M	C	C	R	I	M	E	S	C	E	N	E
S	L	I	O	P	J	E	O	E	G	Z	E	N	Y	V	U	R	A	W	W
M	N	H	S	E	Z	J	Z	P	Z	M	Q	L	V	P	G	V	D	S	Q
M	P	M	X	C	O	N	T	A	M	I	N	A	T	I	O	N	N	D	N
K	E	G	R	Z	A	G	R	N	T	G	K	K	B	L	D	D	D	T	S
D	U	P	G	L	W	I	Y	P	A	C	K	A	G	I	N	G	A	N	N

Exploring Forensics: Careers for Curious Minds: Pathways for Future Careers.

Forensic Biology

```
S Y C E P Q P L G Z B C Y I S A P C A M
H O X B Y P L Q N L T K T K D M S D U K
J G P E V I D E N C E G X H I H S T Q B
K Q X A Z E G M Z H H F I Q U L J A G O
B I O C H E M I S T R Y B C L X M R D X
V Y T V Y G U E H R B D M R F S I V K Y
Q R J N T S R K M M H H G A Y W B P S N
G Q T O I C Y V J I H P C T D F I D C O
N W Y I L I J U Q L R V B C O L H S G M
I M K T I T S E H H I X B K B A A Y A I
L M S A B S H W P N Z Q M F U N R D R T
I N S N A I U I H Q E U A N J O A L N S
F I J I B T N R X A B T H R T U K K X E
O W F M O A M Q L U J J C A V T T K R T
R U B A R T B Y S W A E R X X H E Z U A
P N C T P S N I V P Z O I X M K A R A F
A N B N X R D K H V B A G J E B S V R L
N E C O C K L L U A L V K G S A D H L D
D V A C T M W L L E X O N E R A T E H T
Z M F Q T G O M R V A G E D A N E S I A
```

Exploring Forensics: Careers for Curious Minds: Pathways for Future Careers.

Forensic Toxicology

```
C N R E D I S T R I B U T I O N B Z X I
J Z G A V L K V H X O Q W B R L B Q H I
S M V I T R E O U S H U M O U R R G W X
I I M M U N O A S S A Y W H H B X H X S
F E C H R O M A T O G R A P H Y G L M J
F E R I G T K X Z D Y I Z T T T M J Y U
X G L X Y C O N C E N T R A T I O N S E
O Z N K K Z R Z P H A R M A C O L O G Y
K F X P A U Z C B I O C H E M I S T R Y
Q E F Q R Q L Y F S B K F E S L A J U I
H Q W H N N B G Q N S I U H N Z K M Q B
W A P D A U E O J O O L G I A X P O Y T
X G F K U U M L T S G G Q Z E P A N A I
I S C X A Q Y O V I D J Y M I V C S X E
D H N E C A M C M O I P B J O S N X Y I
Y B H R Y D I I D P S X Q S U U X Y N Z
A K D L D Z D X L C J Q T C D E R B T K
B V N F Q X V O E H X D F O D N K X Q X
X U X N T V A T N F Q R C T U I G Z O U
D J K S L A B O R A T O R Y Q C I B Y S
```

Exploring Forensics: Careers for Curious Minds: Pathways for Future Careers.

Forensic Nursing

R	J	Y	V	Y	K	S	A	F	E	G	U	A	R	D	I	N	G	R	J
I	Z	L	D	H	I	Y	G	Q	Z	R	T	C	Z	V	J	V	X	X	E
R	H	F	J	T	F	H	E	B	U	F	F	B	H	Z	B	V	U	M	R
K	T	B	B	X	Q	J	T	O	Z	D	U	B	I	F	E	H	G	D	O
Q	C	R	C	O	N	S	E	N	T	O	T	Y	J	U	S	H	N	G	P
M	L	Q	A	U	Y	W	W	M	Z	T	T	J	T	R	Z	H	I	P	I
G	E	Y	S	S	M	I	N	T	E	G	R	I	T	Y	M	J	S	V	B
T	Y	R	P	K	V	M	N	U	O	L	B	P	B	I	M	T	R	F	X
P	B	E	W	M	E	L	O	Q	T	W	R	W	O	C	X	N	U	V	Q
V	Z	V	T	E	X	Y	I	Y	M	O	O	O	Z	X	V	E	N	F	J
U	C	O	E	P	X	J	T	P	E	S	A	O	S	K	E	M	C	E	J
N	U	C	Y	S	R	C	A	O	E	Q	H	T	N	D	X	E	I	N	C
W	O	E	Q	T	J	U	T	G	C	A	B	T	M	P	O	T	S	Z	L
R	F	R	B	Q	J	P	N	V	N	A	W	I	L	Y	B	A	N	C	O
Q	A	K	R	N	R	E	E	U	E	K	X	S	P	Q	Z	T	E	W	S
O	F	N	R	H	O	D	M	A	D	V	O	C	A	C	Y	S	R	K	G
A	T	V	V	B	J	C	U	D	I	S	D	X	P	C	Z	H	O	C	B
O	D	Q	T	M	D	H	C	A	V	V	C	M	R	H	I	E	F	N	I
T	T	R	A	U	M	A	O	I	E	C	Y	T	T	B	Y	Z	V	C	B
K	V	Q	D	P	F	W	D	L	X	D	F	U	D	P	J	F	O	M	K

Exploring Forensics: Careers for Curious Minds: Pathways for Future Careers.

Forensic Odontology

F	O	R	E	N	S	I	C	O	D	O	N	T	O	L	O	G	Y	A	B
G	G	L	Y	O	P	B	K	K	L	D	N	T	O	L	J	L	S	I	V
C	H	K	B	N	V	R	E	S	T	O	R	A	T	I	O	N	S	Z	Y
B	Y	N	K	M	E	K	M	R	A	D	I	O	G	R	A	P	H	S	M
J	U	G	D	A	A	J	I	R	T	E	R	W	J	L	J	M	B	A	T
R	S	Z	B	W	G	I	R	S	R	N	A	G	I	D	L	G	L	T	L
P	B	D	E	U	W	V	K	X	L	V	U	I	L	U	Q	K	R	L	O
B	Y	T	O	S	O	L	V	F	Q	D	L	W	H	O	B	V	Q	F	C
K	Z	U	Q	J	T	E	B	J	Q	J	B	G	Z	G	N	Z	J	A	O
R	E	S	I	L	I	E	N	C	Y	L	W	O	M	G	O	C	M	B	T
I	D	E	N	T	I	F	I	C	A	T	I	O	N	O	B	T	R	R	O
O	M	G	X	U	M	A	H	O	B	I	T	E	M	A	R	K	S	B	R
I	S	D	C	B	P	H	E	J	G	R	P	E	V	B	Z	U	D	E	P
F	V	J	C	H	A	R	T	I	N	G	H	W	M	Y	V	K	Z	O	X
N	G	D	I	S	A	S	T	E	R	V	I	C	T	I	M	C	O	Q	D
N	V	C	G	P	E	X	H	C	S	H	T	E	E	T	H	U	T	B	W
X	F	A	Y	T	I	Q	R	W	I	C	U	I	J	C	U	I	B	V	V
A	M	X	J	X	P	V	P	V	S	M	F	M	E	U	R	H	B	G	F
X	R	Y	W	Y	Y	Q	W	T	O	L	Q	Q	Y	W	P	V	Z	M	I
P	Q	I	Y	U	Z	Y	D	C	V	G	K	R	K	M	W	N	F	O	V

Exploring Forensics: Careers for Curious Minds: Pathways for Future Careers.

Forensic Psychology

```
Y J H Z W B T W E S N N O Y X W Z U B Q
D S R Y P I K E Y F W U T Z A I E N Z G
M U U S D W R I G S N I D Y D B K F C H
S A J C J O T V O T F O L X N D A P K R
I A R I Y J E R L T P M D H N M U Q N W
V Q B H T C F E O C X U W J X F T E N N
I J X T I V N T H W U G I V U S T U V Y
D R P E L Y F N C L Q B D F F T K Y R Y
I T G C A O Z I Y E R P N J Z W X O A K
C N T X I M W R S C Y A V J Y P M J T S
E E J N T Q L F P N N C K Q S E G E K B
R M X D N B M H C E O C G B M R W L L O
D S Q B E R N X I T M X K F I Y W X Y X
B S S H D W K S S E I U T L M E X O Y V
X E V P I Q X V N P T X R P D P B V O S
Z S R C F Q E E E M S W G M G I S P K T
C S K T N Z A D R O E S E Q T C N Y O A
Z A V J O K R V O C T L T V J N Y D J W
A P B S C C B Z F T F C X H A W K I X R
H M S K K L M E Y E W I T N E S S W B Y
```

103

Exploring Forensics: Careers for Curious Minds: Pathways for Future Careers.

Forensic Accounting

```
L H O C U X Y B O U U G V F D K W I Q V
Z O O S Q C O N T R O L S L D I N C C W
L D A T A A N A L Y T I C S N X H B Y P
R Q S Y W H V A R P R Q N F G N Q Q D X
J F N W I H E L X J Y P Q N W T H Z G Y
S F A W M P X S Z Z Z I S U P O P W C
K W D S B S A D Q B M T B E O J S A C N
F S D B Z N Z P U P R S C Q G W M I S E
R Q Y V I S S C C O L N F S E K V Y P R
J Q D F N M W G P V E N N I K Y G D W A
C B S H H A G E H D S O V Y I T H U C P
M R X T X W R J I D I R M S W I N A O S
G D A D C Q E V H T E J J D V V F R P N
X S M S N A E M C T X D I I C I H F Y A
A U D I T E S A N V Z D A F G T H W S R
V K Z M G W S I E M H D R X T C B L H T
T A Q Y Y N B A F J F C U M D E H F Z Y
O M L I A X O O C H V B E B P J U P M X
H P X R V P E J N O H L L P M B N K E H
L N T C H P Y H O T X S M D I O C E A E
```

PART III:

CAREER LAUNCH AND GROWTH

Building Your Portfolio and Professional Identity

A good portfolio demonstrates both competence and dedication to the profession of forensics. Start with University or training school projects. Case reports, laboratory analyses, and research posters demonstrate technical ability and discipline in completing tasks. Where possible, include examples of mock witness statements or expert reports that adhere to professional formats.

Short courses add weight. Taking workshops on how to handle evidence, courtroom skills, or specialised techniques shows that you are putting what you learnt in school into practice. Conferences and professional meetings are great places to share research, learn more, and meet people who might hire them. Make sure to keep track of who comes and goes, as well as any presentations or posters. This demonstrates your involvement with the broader forensic community.

An online presence can help establish your identity if done carefully. A professional profile on networks such as LinkedIn should emphasise education, certifications, and most importantly, projects without revealing sensitive information. Be cautious when discussing casework or showing pictures; privacy is of utmost importance. A good digital footprint can help potential employers feel better about hiring you because it shows that you know how to stay within the law as well as how to do your job.

Finding Roles and Succeeding at Interviews

Vacancies are available in public agencies, private laboratories, consulting companies, academic institutions, and other organisations. Monitor the career pages of police forces, forensic providers, regulatory bodies and scientific organisations. Professional societies and university career

Exploring Forensics: Careers for Curious Minds: Pathways for Future Careers.

services are often the primary sources of opportunities that are circulated before they reach general job boards.

Make each application unique. Use specific examples of your relevant experience, like field placements, lab work, or research projects, to make your CV and cover letter fit the list of skills in the ad. Focus on skills that can be applied in various jobs, such as collaborating with others, thinking critically, and communicating effectively with people. These are the most important skills for forensic jobs.

Interviews may include assessment centres, scenario questions, or real-life tasks. Learn the basics, including the chain of custody, maintaining cleanliness, and making ethical decisions. Practice breaking down complicated processes into simple terms; many panels have people who aren't scientists on them. Behavioural questions often begin with "Tell us about a time when." Use the STAR method: Situation, Task, Action, Result, to organise your answers clearly. Sometimes, being able to think clearly and make professional decisions is just as convincing as having technical knowledge.

Exploring Forensics: Careers for Curious Minds: Pathways for Future Careers.

Continuing Professional Development and Networks

You have to keep learning for the rest of your life if you want to work in forensics. To stay up to date on the latest in technology, law, and best practices, read professional journals and good online bulletins on a regular basis. Connect with others at seminars, webinars, and local chapter meetings to share ideas and build connections. Ask your boss or a professional association for advice on career paths and specialised training. Keep a reflective log to document new skills and pinpoint gaps and establish annual development plans to keep development measurable. Active participation in these networks not only supports competence but it is also indicative of the curiosity and adaptability that is celebrated throughout the forensic sciences.

**Exploring Forensics: Careers for Curious Minds:
Pathways for Future Careers.**

PART IV:

CAPSTONE LEARNING TOOLS

CASE MATRIX ACROSS CAREERS

Career (Case)	Key Evidence Types	Principal Risks	Outcome / Learning Point
Forensic Anthropology – historic remains	Skeletal profile, trauma marks, soil context	Loss of context, taphonomic change	Identity inferred despite centuries-old remains; shows value of scene archaeology.
Forensic Pathology – unwitnessed death	Autopsy findings, histology, toxicology	Post-mortem change, sample mix-ups	Natural cardiac death confirmed; illustrates correlation of medical history with autopsy.
Crime Scene Investigation – burglary series	Latent prints, footwear, trace DNA	Scene contamination, chain-of-custody errors	Integrated evidence linked suspect to multiple sites.

Exploring Forensics: Careers for Curious Minds: Pathways for Future Careers.

Forensic Biology – sexual assault kit	DNA profile, semen detection	Secondary transfer, partial profiles	Database hit secured conviction; expert emphasised statistical limits.
Forensic Toxicology – therapeutic drugs	Blood, urine, vitreous humour	Post-mortem redistribution	Drugs ruled incidental; careful interpretation avoided false poisoning claim.
Forensic Nursing – SARC exam	Injury photographs, swabs, patient statement	Consent withdrawal, re-traumatisation	Survivor received care and evidence preserved for later decision.
Forensic Odontology – air disaster	Dental charts, radiographs	Record gaps, bias in comparison	Teeth provided definitive identification where DNA was destroyed.
Forensic Psychology – fitness to plead	Cognitive tests, structured interviews	Over-interpretation of behaviour	Court received balanced opinion with clear limits.

Exploring Forensics: Careers for Curious Minds: Pathways for Future Careers.

Forensic Accounting – procurement fraud	Ledger extracts, emails, bank data	Data loss, incomplete disclosures	Red-flag analytics enabled recovery and control reforms.
Detective Work – robbery series	CCTV, telecoms, witness interviews	Disclosure failures, witness fatigue	Coordinated strategy produced arrest and restored community confidence.

Exploring Forensics: Careers for Curious Minds: Pathways for Future Careers.

Ethical dilemmas for discussion

DNA and Consent

During a cold case review, you find a partial DNA match to a teenager whose DNA sample was taken years ago for an unrelated medical study. Consent for criminal use was never obtained. Police appeal to the court for access, arguing that the public interest takes precedence over privacy. Should you release the data? Under what safeguards?

Digital Evidence and Privacy

You are looking through a suspect's phone as part of an investigation into a burglary and come across some explicit images that appear to be associated with some form of unrelated child exploitation. The current warrant only covers property crimes. Do you stop what you are doing and look for a new warrant or quietly report what you have seen? How do you record the discovery without breaching the procedure?

Exploring Forensics: Careers for Curious Minds: Pathways for Future Careers.

Financial Misconduct Beyond the Brief

Hired to investigate the procurement of goods by a company and discover significant tax evasion by the same company, which is out of the client's instructions and not yet illegal under local thresholds. Do you report to authorities, warn the client privately or stick to the contracted scope?

Interview Pressure

A senior investigator encourages you to employ a confrontational interviewing style to "shake loose a confession." You are of the opinion that it endangers the purity of testimony and violates professional codes. Refusing could hurt the relations between the team and delay the case. How do you reconcile ethical standards of interviewing with the operational demands?

Victim Autonomy

In a sexual assault examination, the survivor agrees to have evidence collected, but later requests that the samples be destroyed for fear of being retaliated against. The law requires the maintenance of evidence once it is collected. Do you follow the statute, or honour the survivor's request and be subject to disciplinary action?

Cultural Sensitivity and Human Remains

Working as a forensic anthropologist, you are asked to excavate some remains from a sacred burial ground to assist in a criminal investigation. The local community is strongly against disturbance. Can you harmonise the needs of justice with cultural respect, and if so, how?

Expert Witness Neutrality

A defence lawyer secretly provides an offer of a consultancy fee to "help them understand weaknesses" in your forthcoming testimony. The fee is generous and legal if declared, but it might undermine the perception of impartiality. Do you accept, refuse, or put stringent conditions?

Exploring Forensics: Careers for Curious Minds: Pathways for Future Careers.

Laboratory Shortcuts

Under a lot of pressure with the caseload, a colleague proposes skipping a second verification step that doesn't often result in mistakes. The threat of contamination is small, but real. Reporting the shortcut could jeopardise relationships and delay outcomes for the families of victims. How do you act?

Public Communication

After a high-profile case, you get asked by the media to comment on your analysis. The court has made a decision, but an appeal is possible. Do you speak to educate the public, or remain silent in order to protect impartiality and the integrity of potential appeals?

Mental-Health Disclosure

While evaluating the fitness of a defendant to plead, you discover suicidal thoughts. Sharing this information could violate confidentiality, but withholding the information could put the person at risk. What is your duty of care, and how do you communicate this?

Exploring Forensics: Careers for Curious Minds: Pathways for Future Careers.

PART V:

CONCLUSION AND NEXT STEPS

You've now travelled through the many landscapes of forensic science: laboratories where one fibre can speak for the dead, courtrooms where measured words determine freedom, and communities where careful evidence collection restores confidence after damage. Each career described in this book, whether it focuses on bones, chemicals, finances or human behaviour, exists for one purpose: to shed light and justice on moments of doubt.

The path you choose will require some skill and perseverance, but above all, it's a public service. Forensic work requires you to put the truth above your own opinion, to treat the smallest sample as if justice itself hinges upon it, and to treat each individual, be it victim, suspect, colleague or witness, with dignity. Science provides you with the tools, but character provides those tools with meaning. Accuracy is empty without integrity; integrity is powerless without accuracy. Both have to co-exist in every action you take.

Exploring Forensics: Careers for Curious Minds: Pathways for Future Careers.

Scientific care is not just the mastery of instruments or perfecting technique. It is a habit of mind: documenting every step, questioning every assumption, and remaining open to peer review. It is that silent discipline of re-checking a calculation once more, stopping before you make a statement in court to make sure that your words are true to the evidence. When you conduct science in this spirit, you become a guardian of reliability, demonstrating to society that facts are something to believe in, despite the emotions running high.

Just as important is the public trust. Every chain of custody that you are maintaining, every report you are writing with a balance of language, solidifies confidence in the justice system. People in your community may never know your name, but they will feel the stability your work brings. Families can grieve with confidence, the innocent can be protected, and the guilty can be held accountable without fear of being wronged when evidence is gathered and explained carefully.

Now is the time to take your next step. Build a professional identity that is founded on curiosity and humility. Find mentors who push you to do better and who are always open to new ideas and technologies. They should also never stop

Exploring Forensics: Careers for Curious Minds: Pathways for Future Careers.

learning after they finish school. Attend conferences, conduct research, and consider each case, not just for technical lessons but also for the human stories they reveal.

Also, remember the importance of balance. Forensic careers can bring violence, loss, and ethics to you. **Protect Your Own Wellbeing as Carefully as You Protect Evidence**. Strong boundaries, supportive colleagues and time for reflection will help keep your service going and your judgement clear.

Forensic professionals who are both precise and caring are needed in the world. Your work can help determine what really happened when it matters most, whether it's standing at a crime scene at midnight, examining a DNA trace, unravelling complex stories, or understanding how a defendant is feeling. Step up in self-assurance for every careful action that will strengthen justice and honour those who depend on it. The charge is simple but profound: serve the evidence, serve the people and let your science be a quiet but persistent force for fairness.

Exploring Forensics: Careers for Curious Minds: Pathways for Future Careers.

ABOUT THE AUTHOR

Shivani Sanger is a PhD researcher in Biological Anthropology and the founder of *Shivani STEM Scholars*, an initiative dedicated to inspiring the next generation of learners and educators in science. She holds a BSc in Biomedical Science (IBMS accredited), an MSc in Forensic Medical Science, and an MSc in Professional Human Osteoarchaeology. With over five years of clinical medical experience, four years in a biomedical science laboratory, and three years working with human remains ranging from modern to archaeological, Shivani brings a wealth of knowledge to her teaching and writing.

Exploring Forensics: Careers for Curious Minds: Pathways for Future Careers.

As the first in her family to pursue higher education, her journey has been shaped by curiosity, resilience, and a commitment to making science accessible to all. Through teaching, writing, and mentoring, Shivani aims to spark curiosity and inspire readers to recognise that breaking new ground is always worthwhile.

~Thank You~

Copyright © Shivani Sanger 2025

www.ingramcontent.com/pod-product-compliance
Lightning Source LLC
Chambersburg PA
CBHW052056070526
44584CB00017B/2208